AN ATHEIST'S
JOURNEY TO THE
CROSS

A Pathfinder's Guide

to the Real Christ

KIRSTIE WELLS

DESTINY IMAGE™ EUROPE srl
Via Maiella, 1
66020 San Giovanni Teatino (Ch) - Italy

"Changing the world, one book at a time!"

This book and all other Destiny Image™ Europe books are available at Christian bookstores and distributors worldwide.

To order products, or for any other correspondence:

DESTINY IMAGE™ EUROPE srl
Via Acquacorrente, 6
65123 - Pescara - Italy
Tel: +39 085 4716623 - Fax: +39 085 9431270
E-mail: info@eurodestinyimage.com

Or reach us on the Internet: **www.eurodestinyimage.com**

ISBN: 978-88-89127-73-5
For Worldwide Distribution, Printed in the U.S.A.
1 2 3 4 5 6 7 8/13 12 11 10 09

DEDICATION

This book is dedicated to those people who will come to know Jesus Christ as their personal Lord and Savior through reading it.

ACKNOWLEDGMENTS

I want to thank everyone who God has used to help me escape from the hell I had been living in and discover the Kingdom of God. They know who they are; but I especially want to thank my twin sister, Pauline, who because of her prayers and stubborn perseverance, helped Jesus to save my life.

In 2003 my twin sister attended the Clan Gathering meeting at St. Andrews, an amazing event held once a year where all denominations in Scotland meet and worship together with invited speakers from all over the world. It was at this meeting that one of those speakers, the well-known American preacher and teacher, John Paul Jackson, gave a prayer call, asking anyone who had a unsaved twin sister or brother to stand up and pray for their twin. My sister was so distraught by the knowledge that I was not saved that she could not even manage to stand up for this special prayer.

When I attended this conference the next year, I met John Paul Jackson and said to him, "Do you remember that prayer call for twins you called out for last year?" He replied that he did. I then said, "Well…I'm one of those twins, and I'm now saved." The look on his face turned to delighted surprise, and he gratefully thanked me for informing him that those prayers had been answered.

I am so delighted too, and I thank God all the time for saving me. Thank You, God the Father, God the Son, and God the Holy Spirit.

ENDORSEMENT

Kirstie Wells' spellbinding journey, from an evangelical atheist to that of an evangelical Christian faith, reminds me why I'm not an atheist. First, I'm too lazy; atheism is such hard work—you have to deny so much. Second, I'm too right-brained—atheism is a massive failure of the imagination. And third—Jesus Christ. Kirstie's story is one you will want to share with your atheist friends. (Please tell me you have some.)

Leonard Sweet
Drew University, George Fox University

TABLE OF CONTENTS

FOREWORD

God is in the business of changing lives. Transformation happens as He reveals Himself through our personal circumstances and we respond affirmatively! Each of us has a story to tell. Scripture reminds us that before we were formed in our mother's womb, God knew us and had a wonderful plan for our lives. However, because of free choice, we may opt not to follow His plan.

Such was the case for Kirstie Wells. Though born into a religious family, her choices led her on a search for fulfillment and happiness in all the wrong places. As she doubted her faith and chose to follow the route of atheism, she worshipped at the altar of self-gratification. Yet when she came to the end of her rope, God was there to provide an opportunity for her to meet Him. Subsequently, because of her choice to accept Him, she found the answer to her great frustration and unanswered questions. God knew how to reveal Himself so that she would truly know Him and believe.

I first became acquainted with Kirstie while conducting leadership training at the seminary where she was studying in Germany. For two consecutive years, following our conferences at the seminary, she served as our guide and driver in France and Holland. As a European, her knowledge of the areas to which we travelled provided us inside information, while her humor, candidness, and tenacity also greatly enhanced our travel experiences. Listening to her share her testimony of life-change and of her relationship with God, and specifically the Holy Spirit, was encouraging indeed!

While we visited Amsterdam in 2007, Kirstie took us on a walking tour that included the small church where her dad once served as pastor. As we stood in front of the church, we heard firsthand the story of how she led her dad to Christ shortly before his death. In this book, she also shares the story of growing up in a pastor's home and dealing with the illness that eventually took her father's life.

I pray that God provides the opportunity for many proclaimed atheists to read of how a former atheist found the solution to her messed-up life. And that solution was the God she had formerly denied.

Tony P. Lane, International Coordinator
Church of God International Department
of Youth and Christian Education
Cleveland, Tennessee

Chapter 1

IT ALL STARTED WITH A VOICE

And God said, Let there be light. And there was light (Genesis 1:3).

Had I previously known what would be in store for my life when Jesus spoke to me a few years ago, I never would have believed it! You see, when I accepted Jesus Christ as my personal Lord and Savior in April 2004, I really didn't have a clue what it was all about! It never dawned upon me at that moment that I would literally be taken *"out of the darkness and into the light."* Even this way of speaking made no sense at all to me!

I had been married to a space satellite contract engineer for nearly 20 years; and while we had been looking into space for all those years, we still continued to read and believe in the supremacy of mankind over all his achievements—real postmodernist belief system stuff. And never once did we see the hand of God in our creation, or in our surroundings, or in our universe.

But all this came crashing down literally on the day when I heard the voice of an invisible presence speaking next to my left ear, on a day when I was contemplating how I would be able to live my life without my husband. My marriage was quickly disintegrating around me, and as I looked at myself despairingly in my bathroom mirror, a voice clearly said:

It'll be all right. It'll be all right.

I turned around in shock to see if there was anyone behind me…but no one was there. With a puzzled frown, I turned back and looked at myself again in the mirror. And then I felt a presence wrap "itself" around my shoulders like a giant mantle. This amazing feeling entered into my whole upper body and lasted for over five minutes. I felt a peace and calmness wash over and through me; and I felt the anguish, pain, and anger literally melt away. As I gazed at myself in the mirror, I saw the expression of despair on my face turn to absolute joy!

This is what this book is all about; this is my testimony years later—a story I want to share with the world.

Chapter 2

My "Enchanted" Existence

So that if any one is in Christ, that one is a new creature; old things have passed away; behold, all things have become new (2 Corinthians 5:17).

So…what happened next? What happens when a person hears a voice coming out of nowhere? How does a "normal" person react?

Well, I know how I reacted! I ran straight down the stairs and out the back door of my home. I don't actually remember what happened immediately after that; I most likely had a large gin and tonic, which was a normal thing to do in those days—that was, after all, part of my life.

At the time, I was living in a small, twee, and cutesy English village made up of one main street leading onto the main thoroughfare, a village that is situated between a local town and a beautiful spa town a few miles away.

The whole vista of the village is of the "old life," consisting of quaint cottages with slate or thatched roofs amongst large Victorian mansions where the rich and the noble lived in a bygone era. Still today, it is only the rich and the relatives of the nobles who live in those large red-brick buildings adorned with classical columns and accompanied by rows of neat hedges and trimmed gardens.

In the well-manicured gardens are bright purple and blue foxgloves and delicate hollyhocks swaying their heads in the breeze. The ivy adamantly clings to the bricks, adding their twisting decoration to the facades of the houses. On a beautiful, humid, and still summer day, the noise of bees humming while gathering honey from the golden-colored and sweet-smelling honeysuckles is most likely the loudest noise a person will hear.

Although the cottages once housed local families who worked at the brickworks and cottage industries, they now accommodate satellite commuters whose salaries can afford to pay the price for living in such a coveted place.

The cottage that we owned and where I lived with my husband sits on the corner of the country road as it enters into the village proper. A few houses down the street is the local pub—The Rose & Crown—where, up until a few years ago, before the hunting ban, the local hunt would meet, sitting proudly on their horses, fully equipped in their hunting outfits—cream-colored jodhpurs, shiny black boots, whips, and hard hats—to sup sherry and port before heading off to chase down the local foxes. The village itself has the obligatory traditional village green, surrounded by even more enchanting little cottages with designer overgrown gardens and terraces. This is the center of village life where elaborate fetes and parties are held to celebrate social events with names like The Wake—a traditional village event with booths and a spit upon which a local farmer's donated pig is roasted and served in a bun with homemade applesauce. Much beverage is consumed, both alcoholic and nonalcoholic, and people come from miles around to partake in the event.

Next to the village green is an old church yard alongside a yellow-stone Norman church. Its graveyard houses the remains of many well-known family members. Inscriptions on the old headstones are almost illegible with patches of moss growing into the carved names and dates, fading away with time.

Next is the football club where the local team plays. Here, during the day, youngsters aspire to be famous football players, while in the evening, the clubhouse turns into a "lad pub," which provides entertainment with strippers and an abundance of ale. Then there is the cricket club where one can sit on the lawn on a hot steamy day among stately tall oaks, sipping Pimm's with ice, lemon, and lemonade, and listening to the crack of the cricket ball against the bats, along with the cheering or jeering, depending upon the shot just played.

Around the corner and across a field from where I lived, there is the local school at the top of the hill, where my goddaughter attended primary school. Likewise, located here is the church hall where the youngsters of the village attend Sunday school and other activities, and where dances and parties are held.

This is the village that I had been a part of for almost 18 years, when we weren't working abroad. It is all very sophisticated, expensive, and "normal" in an un-normal sort of way. It is here that we lived in between European work contracts and holidayed whenever we could—coming home for Christmases, New Years, and summer holidays. I was part of this captivating life where the locals live among their charming homes, social clubs, and the village pub, which I helped to run. I was deeply entrenched in the ways of life where people become crippled by their credit cards, drive their Range Rovers (which are too expensive to run), wear designer Wellingtons and Burberry coats, and where the rich, who although they can afford to live there, remain tight-fisted, refusing to pay local bills for as long as possible.

In this delightful little corner of the country, deep in the heart of Middle England, a voice with an invisible body wasn't supposed to speak to me in my bathroom. In this whimsical setting, I wasn't supposed to be almost dying from an emotional and awful disintegration of my marriage. And up until that point in time, a person called Jesus did not, for me at any rate, exist. He was a complete and utter non-person, a made-up character or myth who, if He did exist, was a meek and mild figure with no guts or substance or reality. He was that name that I swore by; He was that name that I cursed by; He was that person who did not exist—not at all.

I was an atheist. I did not believe in God. Likewise, I was not about to believe in a "Son of God." Although my father and grand-father had been preachers, God still meant nothing to me. I just did not believe, and I had never considered believing. I was a complete atheist, a hedonist, a non-believer. Yes, I had attended church in order to please my father—after all, I was a "daddy's girl." But even so, in all that time, I had never considered his God or his God's Son or what this God could mean to me.

I came from a strict traditional Church of Scotland home where we were taught to be good minister's kids. But if Jesus did exist then, He certainly was too busy and too far away for me. Which is why it was so strange to find out that I knew, just knew, after a few days, that the voice I had heard belonged to a person whom I thought didn't exist. Very soon I would have my mind changed totally and completely because I just knew, from that moment onward, that the voice I had heard belonged to Jesus Christ. It wasn't a slow growing knowledge; it didn't take months for me to figure this out. I became aware very quickly. I knew within a very short time that I had had some sort of amazing experience.

But this experience was nearly wiped out as the situation between my husband and me suddenly intensified and our relationship deteriorated quickly.

Up until that time, if someone had told me that Jesus existed, I would have laughed hysterically. Yet if someone had told me that satan existed, I would have become very angry and told that person to stop being so stupid. There was no such thing as satan—he was a joke, and I would have become haughtily derisive. The devil didn't exist; and even if he did, he was just some character who wore a red suit, grew a tail, and carried a pitchfork in his hand. I would have likened him to the character on the "Tom & Jerry" cartoons where a little devil and a little angel sit on Tom's opposite shoulders tempting him to do the right or wrong thing.

But all of a sudden, in my "Little Red Riding Hood" cottage situated in a highly desirable and sophisticated village in the middle of the English countryside, my life was being stirred up beyond my understanding or knowledge.

Until a person knows what lies behind the tales about satan and realizes that this evil being not only does exist but also hates mankind and wants to kill us all (both Christians and non-Christians, in the most horrendous ways possible), then no one can really understand just how awful this part of my life was. Just as the knowledge of eternal truth was about to be revealed to me, the gates of hell started to work overtime. Of course, at this time, I didn't know that this character existed, nor did I have a clue at the hidden machinations he was using with the intent to destroy me. First and foremost, he was doing everything he could to ruin my life *before* I could be introduced to Jesus. And then, when that didn't work, and subsequently Jesus spoke to me, the devil really "turned the heat up" so that I could not become further acquainted with Jesus.

Because the devil, the father of all lies, constantly bombarded me with trickery and deceit, it would take several years before I came to the full understanding of who Jesus really is and what He means to me. In those first years of torment and uncertainty, Jesus had to reach out to me constantly and on a daily, moment-to-moment basis to save me from being overtaken by the sheer hell of my situation. He is the only reason I am alive to write this book today. Jesus kept me going in the face of all hell breaking loose against the knowledge of exactly who I am in Him.

You, also, can know who you are in Jesus. Indeed, you can realize how to stand as a child of God, and learn how to keep on standing against the adversity coming against you.

Chapter 3

THE FIRST STEP TO
ANOTHER LIFE

*And we know that all things work together for good to those
who love God, to those who are called according to His purpose*
(Romans 8:28).

The end of my atheist life came about four weeks after my encounter with "someone" in my bathroom (who I would later realize
was Jesus Christ). Initially, I had tried to pretend that nothing had
happened…but it didn't work. I just couldn't pretend something
hadn't happened which actually had happened!

Then, matters got worse when I spoke to my twin sister, a born-
again Christian, living in Scotland. She knew that my relationship
with my husband had been desperately in need of help; and consequently, she and her church were actively praying for me as my marriage was falling apart. But every time we spoke and she tried to talk
to me about Jesus, I would scream at her and slam the phone down.
Yet I knew I had to talk to someone.

So, finally, after a couple weeks, I called her husband, Steve, and
told him what had happened. His response, likewise, was not what I

wanted to hear—"You know it's Jesus." This time, instead of slamming the phone down, I started to sob. Life was hellish and I could no longer function properly.

Two weeks later, on a Sunday evening, a humdinger of arguments occurred between me and my husband, which would mean the end of our relationship. He had already been working away from home every week; so the next morning, as usual, he drove away without saying good-bye. I then tried to take hold of my situation. Fortunately, God was already ahead of me.

On that Monday, I cried and cried as I spoke with my family on the phone. My parents agreed with me that I had done all I could and that it was time for me to leave. In my heart of hearts, I was hoping that simply saying I was going to leave would jolt my husband into some sort of reconciliation. Then, the next day, Tuesday, when I walked into work, I discovered that my job was no longer available. I had been working in a tourist office helping to organize holiday concerts worldwide, but the head of staff had decided the overheads were too high and I got the "chop." So, by Wednesday, March 30, 2004 having no reason to stay any longer, I packed and left home.

I literally took everything of personal significance from my cute little cottage home, jammed it all into the car, and drove away. Everything that had had any meaning to me after 20 years of living with my husband was in that vehicle. There was only one person in the village who knew I was leaving, and she was my next-door neighbor who had gone through the entire marriage breakdown with me. However, the one detail I had not revealed to her was my encounter with the invisible Son of God; she wouldn't have believed me then…and she still doesn't now.

So I ran away from home, all the way from the Midlands of England to the north of Scotland, to my twin sister's home. Four days later, I arrived at her house on April 2—the date of our birthday. Both my sister and I remember my arrival in a huge 4x4 jeep full of all my stuff, including a huge brown and cream teddy bear, named Sampson, and all my toys on the front seat. I literally fell out of the car with exhaustion but with a smile on my face, shouting, "Happy Birthday!" The stress of the last two years of my marriage break- down had left me at the point of mental exhaustion, and the initial relief was huge.

The drive from what had been my home situated in the coun- tryside south of Birmingham to Lossiemouth, a small town on the northeast of Scotland, had been amazing. My 4x4 had literally flown up the motorways of England, up through the beautiful areas of the north where I decided to stop for one night at a small town in the Lake District. There I found a small hotel and started chatting with a kind gentleman who had dinner with me and es- corted me to the door of my room afterwards, where we politely said goodnight. I now know that he was God-sent, to look after me on that first night on my way to discover who Jesus really was. Was he an angel? Perhaps.

Two days after my arrival, my sister then invited me to her Pen- tecostal church on Sunday. At that service, she asked me if I would like to know Jesus as "my personal Lord and Savior," and I said, "Yes." I wept for what seemed to be hours and hours. The sheer re- lief at taking the first step onto the road of this new life with Jesus was amazing. I was surprised at how moving it could be. Two weeks later, I was baptized, and shortly after that, I received the baptism of the Holy Spirit and the gift of speaking in tongues. And that was when the "fireworks" really started.

At the beginning, while adjusting to living in my sister and brother-in-law's home, I kept holding onto the hope that my husband and I would be able to reconcile; but he was adamantly against any form of reuniting. I now understand why, but at that time, I wasn't aware of how much "the dark hates the light." Still, I wanted to learn about this new reality of Christ.

Previously, ever since I was of the age to form my own opinion, I had decided that I didn't believe in God or Jesus. As a child, my read- ing material had been adventure and fantasy stories. And when I met my husband, an engineer working in the space satellite industry, I was then introduced to his favorite subject, which became my bible and my belief system—science fiction and fantasy, which neatly fit into my life. This belief system had been my reality, which was then developed and shaped by Renaissance humanism, Victorian modernity, and Enlightenment postmodernity, all centering on the superiority of mankind. No place for God at all.

Shortly before I left my husband, I had just finished studying with the Open University, a secular long-distance learning university, and had been awarded a Bachelor of Arts degree in History. These courses took me from fifth century B.C. Athens up to and including post Second World War II literature, encompassing existentialism, philosophy, and religion. I can now see the hand of God in every one of the courses I chose, as the range of literature encompassed historical criteria, which is necessary to know in subjects such as the history of religion worldwide. I studied the early Greek myths and legends, the religious arts and poetic language of the Renaissance alongside its religious political farce, through the entire period of the Reformation in a course titled "1450–1600 Culture and Belief in Europe," and then into the Victorian and Enlightenment periods, culminating in the existentialism of Sartre and his peers at the end of World War II.

I had been taught at school that man had evolved from apes, and I believed, totally and completely, that this was true. I believed in "survival of the fittest," and I believed that mankind needed to "move out into space" as a real and certain answer to the dilemma of the population explosion on earth and the increasing problems caused by global warming. The solution of putting men into tin cans in space, as well as living in domed cities on Mars, seemed very acceptable ways to escape overcrowding. I was able to justify, quite literally, the spending of billions of dollars to send man into space rather than give money to the poor and starving on planet Earth. My belief and my faith was that we ourselves could save mankind. I looked out into space with my space consultant engineer husband through his mega telescope and never saw Jesus. I never saw a God who could have created this amazing universe. No God. No Jesus. Very simple.

But when my world crumbled and fell apart, Jesus came and rescued me. Just as He did for the Samaritan woman at the well, Jesus caused a deliberate diversion to occur in my life, and He came and saved me. This is why I am living completely and utterly for Him today. God does answer prayer.

Chapter 4

MY WORLD TURNED
RIGHT SIDE UP

In whom the god of this world has blinded the minds of the un-believing ones (2 Corinthians 4:4a).

On the surface, my entry into God's Kingdom was amazingly un-complicated, largely because the Pine Tree House Community Church welcomed me so lovingly into their church family. Located on the out-skirts of the small Scottish town of Elgin, not far from Lossiemouth, situated in a council housing and industrial area, this church helped me begin my new life as a believer.

After their initial shock at seeing how alike I am to my twin sis-ter, not only in looks but also in speech, they literally took me into the bosom of the family of God. They helped me, they hugged me, they looked after me, and they applauded God when I, along with others including my brother-in-law, went forward for baptism. But underneath there was a real battle going on.

Although I kept telling people that my world had been turned upside down by this wonderful Jesus intervention, I now know that

Jesus was really turning my world right side up. My head had literally been buried in the sand.

For years, I had watched all kinds of scary movies, horror films, and fantasy films like *Harry Potter* and *Lord of the Rings*—nothing hard-core, just amusing…or so I thought. I joined in holiday celebrations on Halloween Eve with the kids dressed up as ghouls and witches. It was, after all, just a laugh—wasn't it? Evil spirits and demons didn't really exist—did they?

They do exist, not as witches and ghouls, but as demons and evil spirits, possessing and oppressing people who then dress up as witches and ghouls. I now understand that many people do not know that they have been totally blinded by the "god of this world," just as I was once fooled. But whether you believe or not, this is serious business; there are those people who serve these invisible invaders from the spirit realm. And unless you have met and know Jesus, you will remain "in the dark" and continue to be deceived by the evil spirits who rule this world. In my own personal life, to recognize that the spirit world actually exists was a real shock to my system—literally and profoundly.

Initially, I was quite surprised to discover that Jesus really existed; so, can you imagine the nightmare shock I experienced when I had my first encounter with demons? No one had told me about this stuff—ever. This was the big lie behind all the little lies—the snare, the bait of satan that modern sophisticated mankind, of whom I was a devoted member, is too clever to believe.

During the next phase of my life, which was tough enough through the ongoing divorce proceedings, I was also undergoing the process of "being delivered" from the pit of hell—a place that I thought didn't exist, along with God, Jesus, and satan. Some people think that satan or hell is something to be made fun of or to be used in a comedy routine as a joke, referring to "having a great party down there." But reality is, there is no party time for mankind in hell. And yes, hell does exist—I've been there.

The Christian who has an easy transition from being a non-believer to a believer is extremely blessed! For me, this was the beginning of the fight of all fights. I suffered through such experiences as seeing flashing lights; at other times, when I looked into a mirror, my face would start turning from black to white as spirit demons tried to frighten me to death—literally. Things were running up and down inside my legs; I felt strange manifestations throughout the rest of my body; and flickering flames circled the top of my head. These manifestations didn't just happen at nighttime; I was under attack 24/7—every moment of the day.

I would be sitting and watching television when strange lights and sparkling clouds would interrupt my watching. Voices and thoughts constantly besieged my mind, and these interruptions could become physical, as I would be jabbed with invisible sharp spikes. At this point, I also started receiving visions from God. One of the first pictures I saw was me being fished out of the broad road that leads to hell. (We can choose one of two roads—the wide road of satan or the narrow road of Jesus.) I saw a huge fishing net dipping into a mass of people on this road. These people, made up of every creed and color, were heading in one direction. The net went down into this mass of people and came back up with me at the bottom of it.

Next I saw myself being dumped literally on the steep side of this road and then sitting next to a big black man. The next vision I had was of me looking down at my feet and noticing that I was standing on a grill. Underneath the grill was a huge black dog viciously snarling and salivating, attempting to attack me. When I later spoke to my father on the phone about this vision, he actually sighed and said, "Oh, yes, that dog—satan." Now, my father didn't talk about the spiritual realm, but he obviously knew what the dog was. I could hear him getting fatherly angry at my treatment when I told him what was going on, but he couldn't help me.

I then realized that these visions were from God, and I started to understand what was going on; God had rescued me through His Son, Jesus, and I was being shown what was happening in the spiritual realm. The real downside was that no one in my church had encountered such extreme demonic manifestations, so they didn't know how to help me; and some people didn't even believe me. So not only was I going through horrendous divorce proceedings at the time, but I was also suffering from lack of deliverance with very little guidance from my Christian family.

Even my twin sister, who dearly loves me but was dealing with own problems at the time, had to deny me help. She became so stricken with my complaining about these "happenings" that one night she informed me that I could not wake her up when I asked if I could do so if something happened. That night, I nearly died of fright; the demonic attack was so intense! She now understands better, and we are each other's prayer partners. However, at that time, many people thought these accusations were "all in my mind," and they determined that I was having a breakdown because of the stress I had experienced during the previous years, in addition to all the years of recreational drug abuse. But the reality was, Jesus needed to extract me from an evil pit, even if my church family didn't understand.

It wasn't long before God mercifully sent help in different forms. First, I met a teacher from the Bible seminary, which I would soon attend, who started the process of deliverance I so badly needed. This man of God came to teach and preach at our church, and during a break, was called to my sister's house by our concerned pastor. The teacher knew immediately what was personally happening to me and took his authority in the name of Jesus over the demon tormenting me. Within a short time, something nasty was kicked out of its old home—me; and I literally saw, through my "spiritual eye," a green, ghoulish, sneering imp leaving my body. There is nothing funny about imps. They might look like the make-believe hobgoblins and dwarf statues that we place in our gardens, but they are deadly and they are dangerous. If, like me, you are familiar with the *Lord of the Rings* or that genre of fantasy adventure, then you actually know what these creatures look like.

At this point, I was asking, "Why am I going through all of this?" Today, I realize that Jesus was with me on this road to deliverance, but at the time it was a terrible experience. I now understand that for some of us, it takes time when we are brought over from the world kingdom to the Kingdom of God. New Christians might have to go through a process where all the lies and indoctrinations we have believed as non-Christians have to be removed. It's like peeling an onion, where layer upon layer of lies are removed one at time. And just as when we peel an onion, we weep as the "Truth" is revealed. The "skin" that holds the juices of the onion within can either be pierced or gently torn off, but either way, the lies will come out and be revealed in the light of Jesus. The key to surviving this spiritual experience is to keep praising God at all times. David the psalmist wrote in Psalm 34:

> *I will bless Jehovah at all times; His praise always shall be in my mouth* (Psalm 34:1).

But it's not always easy to praise God when you are a young Christian being "de-slimed" from satan's filth. Satan is determined that the new Christian should keep his attention on himself so that there is no hope of seeing who he is as a real heir of God. A great help is reading books like *The Screwtape Letters* by C.S. Lewis, who writes from the perspective of a demon trying to keep one of its human charges from getting to know Jesus and thereby being saved. Even C.S. Lewis had to take time out to recover after writing this book, such is the seriousness of demonology.

Meanwhile, the situation with my husband was escalating, and he was insisting on a divorce that he wanted me to initiate on the grounds of "mental cruelty." I had to drive up and down the United Kingdom twice in this time to visit a solicitor in Winchester and my parents who live in the south of England. The journeys were incredible. I was so on fire (and still am) for Jesus that I sang praise songs, spoke in tongues, and blessed as many people driving in their cars as was possible on these trips—all the way from the north of Scotland to the south of England. Surely, many people must have encountered God through my intercessory prayers because of these two journeys!

However, the emotional situation was almost unbearable, and I simply was not up to meeting my husband. On one of the two trips I took to Winchester, he allowed me stay over in our house on my journey as he was still working away from home. This invitation, however, did not turn out to be much of a blessing. In the middle of the night, I was attacked in bed by something black crawling up my legs!

The next day, as I was leaving and standing in what had been my kitchen for 20 years, God showed me the torment and abuse that unsaved mankind continually suffers from. I felt the oppression and sheer hatred of the spirits around me. They absolutely and intensely hated my guts and despised my deliverance out of their realm and into the realm of Jesus. The malice and contempt were tangible—and was what I had been living with and surrounded by for years.

As I walked away from what had been mine—my house, my home, my life, I decided to practice what I had seen an American preacher do on television at my sister's home. He had been teaching on the authority we have over the devil and demons. As a child of God, each of us should know who we are and what we are through His Son, Jesus. In this knowledge, I had my first "proper go" at using my authority in Jesus, and in His name, I turned around on those demons and royally commanded them to "go to hell." In the name of Jesus, I bound every one of them with the authority and power that Christ gives to me through the cross.

Moreover, during this same time period, I also experienced my first spiritual encounter with divine healing. Again, I had been watching a television program where people were receiving healing at a Holy Spirit meeting. As I was observing these healings with a sceptical "Oh yeah" reaction, I suddenly decided to change my attitude and see how it would feel to believe that healings could actually be real. This decision changed my perception immediately. At one point, as I watched a woman laying hands on people, I became so enthusiastic that I jumped up, saying, "I want to do that!"

God heard me, and my schooling had begun.

Chapter 5

TAKING A DETOUR AND MISSING THE TRUTH

So that the light of the glorious gospel of Christ (who is the image of God) should not dawn on them (2 Corinthians 4:4b).

Why is it that we cannot see the truth about who Jesus really is? First and foremost, the god of this world doesn't want us to. We actually belong to satan until we actively cross over the line from the kingdom of hell to the Kingdom of God. So the less the world knows about Jesus, the better. Satan accomplishes this feat in many ways. One of the methods used is religion itself. What better way to keep the truth of Jesus hidden from people than by using their own man-made religions against themselves.

When I first met my husband, I had been living with my parents in Amsterdam where my father was the minister for the Church of Scotland in that city, tending to the English speaking community, made up of both Scots and the Dutch Reformed denominations. The church building is still ever so quaint and situated in the heart of Amsterdam in a small, cloistered area, surrounded by walls, and cut off from the Dam and the Calverstraat, in the heart of the old university area.

I had just finished a gap year in France, where I had been working as an au pair, when my parents invited me to live with them again until I decided what I wanted to do next. I had agreed to go to Dutch language classes with a girlfriend and that is where I met this long black-haired, black-bearded, hippy Englishman. We teamed up and within a short time were living together in a typical Amsterdam, liberal, hedonistic lifestyle paid for by his consultant's wage and my wages from the British Consulate where I worked as a passport, visa, and front office clerk.

My mother absolutely despised this man, while my father was resigned to my decision to go off and live with him. As I was packing up my belongings at my parents' home to go off with my boyfriend, something strange happened, which I would later recall after my conversion. I was clearing my desk and while doing so, I glanced at myself in a mirror leaning against the wall. I stopped short and looked at myself for what seemed a long time, staring into my eyes. I thought I saw something strange in my right eye! As I started to lean forward to look closer, a thought came to me that I should get on with packing my stuff or I would be late for my date. I shrugged at myself and got back to the important business of finishing the packing. This moment would later turn out to be one of great significance.

This was a very difficult time for my parents, especially because my father held an official ministerial position in the mainstream churches of the Netherlands. Not only did he represent the Church of Scotland but he was also the head of the presbytery for the Church of Scotland in Europe—and his daughter was living in sin. And at this time, many nasty affairs were happening at the church, including the fact that the session clerk was having a private nervous breakdown, which he didn't reveal until the church was so badly split that reconciliation was almost impossible.

Although I chose to remain on the outside of all the drama. I still went to church because I loved my dad, whose nickname for me was "Special K." I continued to pay lip service to the church for his sake, but I never understood what dad was preaching about. It went straight over my head. I knew I was lacking "something," but yet life was too interesting to take time to actually look for what was missing. And as the problems in the church increased and my relationship with my new boyfriend developed, I decided to walk away from those Christians who were causing my dad so much grief. I didn't consider the additional pain I might have been causing him and my mum. I just "got out of the sinking boat" and consequently left behind what might have been a possible meeting or point of contact with Jesus.

Instead, I stepped out into the brave new world with this exciting engineer who was working at the cutting edge of space exploration. In addition, I was gobbling up science fiction stories galore with the hedonistic lifestyle that Amsterdam can offer.

Prior to meeting my boyfriend, I had already been introduced to smoking cannabis and then moved on to other mind-altering drugs, including my near-miss heroin addiction. Specifically, I "chased the dragon" in a dirty flat on the east side of Amsterdam, which resulted in my throwing up violently, which in turn convinced me to avoid that nasty trap. Nevertheless, many years of dabbling in recreational or "fun" drugs, such as magic mushrooms, LSD, cocaine, and excessive partying had already started me on a road of several addictions. Moreover, both of us continued to smoked cannabis, which is legal in many European countries, and cigarettes, and drank copiously.

Meanwhile, I continued to work at the consulate and enjoyed life. Our relationship was fiery; we both had competitive and outgoing natures and seldom lived at peace with each other. But, so what? It added zest to life, or at least so I thought at the time.

After a couple of years, my boyfriend was asked if he would work as a consultant on the European Space Plane project in Italy. He jumped at the offer; this was the real thing—working on getting mankind off the planet and into space! We decided to get married to make things easier for us in a Catholic land. (How naive we were.) And then we headed off to Torino in *la bella Italia,* to work for the Italian Space Division.

We loaded up our Volkswagen Transporter outside our tall Amsterdam apartment building, with its gable hook dangling high above us, packing all our worldly possessions, including two little zebra finches called Pinky and Perky in their cage. We were heading for fresh new pastures of exciting space exploration, and this would be the first of our journeys as international space engineer gypsies.

But what a lie we believed! In hindsight, this is still not easy to say—but as part of the Star Trek generation where space in the "final frontier," what a lie we believed. This naive notion that we are in control of our destinies is why Jesus had to come and die for us in the first place. He had to pay for our mistake of accepting satan as our comrade, while denying and rejecting God, our true Friend and Creator.

As we drove happily off to a new life in Italy, we weren't aware, and my ex-husband still isn't aware, of the sheer hell of our reality— the reality that I would have to deal with 22 years later as my pastor shipped me off to a special retreat called Glyndley Manor for more healing and deliverance from the filth that I had picked up during those years of searching.

You see, when I accepted Jesus into my life, He helped me to cross that line that took me from the kingdom of satan to the Kingdom of God. Jesus led me onto this new path; however, I had to be "de-slimed," and the only way to accomplish that was to get to know an awesome person—the Holy Ghost!

Oh, what a Savior we have in Jesus!

Chapter 6

BEGINNING TO STAND

Therefore take to yourselves the whole armor of God, that you may be able to withstand in the evil day, and having done all, to stand (Ephesians 6:13).

Fast-forwarding 22 years, it would be through my pastor in Scotland that I would receive the second form of relief that Jesus sent for me. God made it clear to my pastor that I needed even more help; consequently, he suggested that I go to Glyndley Manor, to a healing and deliverance school, managed by a God-established ministry called Ellel.

The mansion, Glyndley Manor, is set in the beautiful countryside of Sussex on the southern coast of England, close to Eastbourne and in the historical land of the Norman Invasion of Harold the Great, who was killed by a stray arrow that pierced his eye in 1066. Dotting the landscape and identifiable by their distinctive white funnel chimneys, the old hop drying Oost farmhouses peep out of hidden hollows in a captivating countryside. The tall oak and beech trees tower majestically over the landscape, while sheep lazily chew in the surrounding fields.

As I drove down the country lanes lined with high messy hedgerows full of colorful creepers (as well as hidden police speed-trap cameras), I was thinking to myself, as I had done so often before and still do—*How can such a beautiful reality also be so horrendously ugly?* This is one of the saddest realizations I carry—that God made this world for mankind, yet we sold out on God for a lie. These thoughts bring such a sadness whenever I look at God's creation through my eyes with an after-conversion understanding. (And yes, I did get caught speeding by one of those hidden police cameras!)

As I arrived at my destination, I found myself negotiating a narrow driveway into a small haven of rustic peacefulness and formal gardens surrounding the towers of Glyndley Manor. The Ellel Ministry was founded many years ago by an Englishman living in a small village by that name, and this ministry now serves many people all over the world. I was told the miracle story of how God finds these beautiful retreats for this ministry. Here the broken and the wounded can come for help and rest, in addition to learning how to aid others.

For some reason, upon seeing Glyndley Manor, I was also reminded of my previous addiction for science fiction and fantasy, before my conversion. Glyndley Manor is the absolute contrast to the visual experience I had once so enjoyed when watching the Harry Potter films, particularly when the steam train, which Harry and his friends are on, pulls up at the railway station and the students make their way up the dark road to the school of witchcraft called Hogwarts. I used to love the Harry Potter films with the dark and mysterious school of witchcraft and all those amusing adventures of Harry, Hermione, and Ron Weasley.

But now, with the knowledge of Jesus and what is behind these amusing adventures of witchcraft and sorcery, I am no longer enamored with such entertainments; rather, I realize the potential danger behind them. With these influences, satan had messed up my mind and was still messing with my mind so badly that I wasn't able to get hold of my real authority in Jesus Christ. The distractions of demonic interference were keeping my eyes on the dark rather than on the light.

Just as I had done on other journeys, I sang, praised, prayed, and blessed as many people as possible on the drive from Elgin, in northern Scotland, to the Ellel school of healing and deliverance on the coast of southern England. And boy, was I in for an amazing life-changing experience! I do know that conservative Christians, who never experience an attack by demons, find that places like Ellel upset their rationale of Jesus. Yet all I know is that this ministry helped me tremendously when the rationale had failed me completely.

I spent a month at this amazing school learning about the healing and deliverance ministry, based upon correct biblical principles. Each day, we would start with a very acceptable English breakfast and prayers, and then immediately proceed to the first class. Our teachers were a team led by a formidable couple with huge hearts for Jesus and His work for helping people afflicted with addictions, depression, and in need of deliverance from demonic influences. This was the start of my equipping, so that I could go out and help others. It was also at this place that I learned more about the Holy Spirit—who He is, how He is, that He is a real person, and how to work with Him in helping others.

My first head-on encounter with His power was fantastic. We were sitting in a large airy classroom and I had been enduring a cracking headache. As the class began, my sight suddenly went "kaleidoscopic"—very weird stuff. It was as if I was looking out of a kaleidoscope, but there wasn't one there! I told the teacher about it, and he responded, "Okay. Let's just bind it [meaning, immobilize it] in the name of Jesus and see what happens." So he did, and then proceeded with teaching the class.

After a short while, I raised my hand tentatively. The teacher had been giving good instruction, yet I felt it was not good to continue to give time to the devil. The headache had intensified—in fact, my head felt like it was being crushed in a vice! And the kaleidoscope effect was growing worse. When the teacher saw I was in distress, he said, "Okay, class, let's all stop and come alongside our sister." He then started singing a hearty Jesus song to which we all joined in. As we sang, a great weight descended upon the class. An extremely heavy air came down upon the class to the height of our heads and then settled. Later, as it lifted, the pain in my head began to lessen. And suddenly, there was a pinging sensation. Afterwards, the student behind me said that this sensation hit her glasses and then started rising up. I then saw this "thing" flash off, up into the air, where it disappeared. The headache vanished; the kaleidoscope effect stopped; and we resumed the class. It was all so simple in the name of Jesus!

What I now know is that this school is one of God's many schools where His Holy Spirit is the Head Teacher. I also learned that the Bible teaches us that the Holy Spirit would come after Jesus left the earth, to help us, guide us, set us free from our problems, to teach us from Scripture, and to help us to know Him fully. I discovered, very personally, that the presence of God in the person of the Holy Spirit is with us all the time. It is the Holy Spirit who helps set us free from all sorts of bondages and addictions, but He does so only when we are ready. He is a gentle person. And He was instigating my release from demonic oppression while I was sitting in this classroom full of students, seeking help from Jesus and seeking to know Him better.

Sometime after this experience, I was sitting in an old drawing room with a formidable Scottish lady pastor by the name of Jan, whom God used to later direct my next footsteps to a Bible seminary in Germany. It was Jan who showed me how to read the Scriptures as my own personal promises from God. For example, when reading, "The Lord is my shepherd," we would emphasize the personal pronoun "my," bringing home the fact that Jesus is the One who takes care of each one of us.

As we were sitting in this drawing room, I was given the Scripture in the Book of Deuteronomy (chapter 6) about the Promised Land and what it means for me. Just as the Israelites had been led into and given their Promised Land by God, I knew God was telling me through this historical narrative that He would do the same for me. He was leading me into His promised land. But to get there, I would need to travel the road that He had prepared for me. Just like the Israelites, I would have to learn how to walk on that road through many dangers. Those dangers would include facing situations where I would have to learn how to take my authority forcefully. Jesus describes how to gain this authority in Matthew 11:12, in order to realize who I truly am in Jesus Christ.

When I first came to Jesus, my twin sister said that the angels were celebrating in Heaven and that all would be well with me now that I was in the Kingdom of God. And she was right. But what I didn't know, and what so many others don't understand, is that there is a fight, that there is an almighty struggle occurring in the spiritual realms for each one of us. As we mature as Christians and become better acquainted with Jesus, we must first be equipped and then must participate in the battle. There is no choice in the matter; to be effective in the Kingdom of God, we have to stand alongside Jesus against the forces of evil. This is what it means to be "on fire for God."

I have learned, during these last few years, what is meant by "taking a stand." The battle belongs to the Lord; He is our Leader and Captain, and we have our part to play, which is to stand firm in the faith and belief that God gives us once we ask His Son into our lives. That is what I have learned through my experiences. But on that day, sitting in an airy, comfortable drawing room, in an old manor house in the quintessential English countryside, I had no idea of just how dirty this battle really was, and would be.

At that time, I was a mere spectator, being tossed to and fro in the battle of satan versus Jesus. At this point of my journey, satan was still occupying the upper part of the mind battle, and Jesus the lower. But the truth is, Jesus is infinitely higher above the position of satan. I just had to take a hold of this truth. The enemy constantly tries to maintain his status on the high road and cast Jesus down to the low road. New and mature Christians alike should grasp the understanding that getting to know Jesus comes first. Matthew 6:33 states, "But seek first the kingdom of God and His righteousness; and all these things shall be added to you." When I started putting Jesus first in all things, then and only then, did a breakthrough start. And I soon discovered the only way to get to know Jesus is by reading the operating manual of the Kingdom of God—the Bible. Then everything else falls into place. It is very simple, but we humans tend to make it complicated—with the help of the devil.

It was also in this English tea-and-biscuit drawing room that the first indication that the rest of my life was not going to be spent in Scotland dawned upon me. I had left the bonny shores of my birth-land in 1979, at the age of 18 after finishing my secondary education and then went to live in Paris as an au pair for a year. Then, after meeting my husband, I spent most of my adult life either living on mainland Europe or in our home in England. I did not return to live in Scotland until the year that I met Jesus in 2004. Consequently, I had stopped considering this land as my home, although there was still a sentimental pull that only a special country like Scotland can hold.

Upon my return to Scotland, I had been accepted by Aberdeen University to study a teacher's training program in Modern Studies and History through my Open University degree in History. This course was to start in September. However, while sitting with Glaswegian Jan, whose home and parish is in Australia, she looked at me, smiled, and asked, "So you want to be history teacher, do you?" I looked at her and answered, "Well, yes…umm…uhh…I suppose so."

But I had also been talking a lot about the theological seminary in Germany, which I had visited for a week before coming to Ellel. This was the Bible seminary where the teacher, who had exorcised the first demon from me, had come from; subsequently, I had taken a counselling course there and fallen in love with the place. The European Theological Seminary is this amazing old German hotel with a brand-new annex, slotted into place on the side of the old building, a building feat which was completed in seven days! (The story of God creating the world in seven days is a nice reference to this accomplishment.) The seminary is situated on top of a flat mountain in the Black Forest region of Germany, which overlooks the plains of lower France. The average age of the students is between 20 to 25 years old, and what an experience it had been, being with all those young students "on fire" for Jesus.

During that week, I had attended a mission's service at the Volks Missions in the beautiful town of Freudenstadt, the seminary's local town. At that service, during the worship time led by a Russian praise team, I felt a change in the air as I was singing with my eyes closed. When I opened my eyes wondering what was going on, I noticed that the room was full of what looked like red golden rain. I stared at the glory of the Lord in absolute amazement! I asked the campus pastor standing next to me if he could see this sight. He opened his eyes briefly, and said, "Nope...but enjoy." I felt myself grinning inanely. God was especially showing His glory to me—how awesome!

But I didn't realize what God was telling me. I did know that I wanted to go back and study there; but I had already committed to the teacher training course in Scotland and was afraid of losing my place. But with a wee bit more encouragement from Jan, and some interesting international phone calls to the seminary, I decided that it would be a good idea to apply. After phoning the university in Scotland, I discovered I could extend my date of acceptance by a year, and I then applied to go to the Bible seminary for a one-year foundation level course. I knew this was the right thing to do—it just felt right!

By the time my stay at Ellel had finished and I had started the long drive back up the motorways of Britain, I knew that I would be going back home to Scotland, but only to pack up and move out once again—back to Europe. This time my companion would not be my husband, as it had been for so many years; rather, it would be the Holy Spirit at my side.

Chapter 7

JOURNEY TO THE MOUNTAINTOP

For you shall go out with joy, and be led out with peace; the mountains and the hills shall break out before you into singing, and all the trees of the field shall clap their hands (Isaiah 55:12).

Four months later, I was heading back down the motorways of the United Kingdom on my way to start a new life in Germany. As I left my home church, one of the young ladies gave me the Scripture of Isaiah 55:12, quoted above. I drove away, laughing, knowing that as I passed by the trees, they were literally clapping their hands. What a send-off! (And doesn't God have a wonderful sense of humor!)

I knew that God had started the process of teaching me at Glyndley Manor in a significant way. Furthermore, in order to prepare for the rigors of a Bible seminary, I had offered my services as a volunteer helper to the Ellel ministry in Scotland for a two-week period before leaving. Like Glyndley Manor, the ministry building (Blaire House) is an old manor house situated in a superb location of the countryside, in the northeast of Scotland amongst the hills and glens of Aberdeenshire. Also like Glyndley Manor, this superb house was selected specially by God for His healing and deliverance ministry. It was once an old hunting lodge built with large airy rooms and set in simple but formal gardens. And at the one end of the gardens was a vegetable garden surrounded by a high wall and strong gates to prevent the entrance of rabbits and deer. It was here that Jesus moved in another amazingly simple way in my life.

Up until that time, I had been a smoker, puffing away at a pack a day since the age of 13. I had been able to stop smoking at the time of my initial conversion but then started up again. Later, when I went to work at Ellel, I wore a nicotine patch on my arm to try and beat the habit because the Bible seminary campus pastor had told me that to join the seminary I would need to stop smoking. As he informed me on the phone of this requirement, I heard him sigh—I don't think he thought I could meet this one last condition. But I stepped out for Jesus, and Jesus stepped out for me!

Later, as I was working at the manor house, Anna, who continues to manage the center, noticed the nicotine patch on my arm. We had a "wee chat" about me trying to kick the habit, and then she looked into my eyes and said, "Well Kirstie, if you want to put your faith in that patch [looking at the patch], and not in Jesus [looking into my eyes]…." Then she sagely smiled and got on with her paperwork. I was startled. This was a novel idea for me and I went off to my duties thoughtfully. An hour later, I took off the nicotine patch and said, "Okay, Jesus. Break this nicotine addiction, please!" And He did! I had no withdrawal symptoms, no cravings, nothing. And that was in 2004!

It was also at this place that I experienced my first taste of spiritual warfare tactics when a group of Americans arrived. They had come as an intercessory prayer group for the G8 summit, which was taking place in Edinburgh. Arriving noisily, this crowd immediately moved into the building to start their prayer campaign in style. Intrigued, I watched as they split into two groups and began the process of asking God's favor for the meeting of politicians deciding European policies. I have to admit, I really wanted to join in, but there was a lot to do in the kitchens—preparing the food, cleaning the rooms, and serving the meals. Meanwhile, I kept an eye on what was going on, asked questions, and learned just by watching and listening. This was my first real taste of spiritual warfare and intercessory power praying, which left an irremovable mark on my insatiable curiosity for the knowledge of the things of God. I was witnessing something here that I wanted to know a lot more about!

So as I started the first leg of my journey to the Bible seminary, I had plenty to think about. And as I drove to Germany via my parents' home in Bournemouth, I was able to travel in a smoke-free car with no cigarettes at all—wonderful. I had cleaned out the car and the ashtrays for the first time since I had gotten the car. A nicely perfumed 4x4 jeep hit the high roads of Scotland for what would be a three-year absence and headed down to the lowlands of England and beyond.

On this journey across the western part of Europe, I met with many interesting situations. First, there was a stop at Bournemouth to say good-bye to my parents, which turned out to be a difficult experience. My father was in the early stages of liver cancer, and I knew he was failing. My mother was bravely coping, but it was really hard to leave my parents behind. Yet they were extremely encouraging; and my father, who was then a retired minister but still ministering with the Anglican Church as a part-time priest, was proud that I, as the third generation of our house, was now serving God. He prayed and blessed me in this new life, passing on the mantle of his ministry to me, as Elijah had done for Elisha.

My father was a tenacious and determined man of God. A very determined man of God, indeed! After having served for 50 years with the Church of Scotland, he was ordained into the Anglican Church by the Bishop of Salisbury and had to be helped to kneel down to receive the ordination and then to get back up on his feet again. He was part of the religious establishment that I had rejected, and I knew that he did not understand, at that time, what Jesus refers to in John chapter 3. My dad would get upset and angry whenever I tried to speak about the baptism of the Holy Spirit; so I had not been able to approach the subject. Yet his own personal encounter with Jesus would happen sooner than either of us knew.

After spending a few days with my parents, they waved me off from the end of the road as I set off to catch the Hovercraft, crossing the English Channel, from Poole Harbour to France.

As I got ready to visit mainland Europe once again, I wasn't too concerned about being back on French soil. In fact, I had lived in France on four occasions; and while I was an international guide, this country was one of my favorite places to take tourists.

My first French life experience was as an au pair in Paris and in the south of France, looking after the grandchildren of an aging wealthy Parisian couple, and then being passed on to one of their daughters to look after her family. When I completed Aberdeen Grammar School at the age of 18, my parents had decided that the experience of a gap year would perhaps calm my feisty character and possibly help me to settle into, and appreciate, university life afterwards.

This had been a very exciting time for me as it was my initial trip away from my family. I had my first taste of how the rich and famous live while observing my patrons, as well as their friends when they visited my employer's huge, decadent, and expensive houses. I learned much about the French lifestyle, including how to bake patisserie (from the maid, Antoinette) at the Isle de Cite apartment in Paris, where the décor included ankle-high carpet piles and an original Renoir hanging on the wall.

Moreover, the obligatory summer trip to the holiday home estate in the south of France introduced me to another French style of living, while a visit to the President's Island and the theater in Toulon was yet another eye-opener into the true French bourgeoisie world of famous reporters and writers—quite a learning opportunity for a wide-eyed 18-year-old. These experiences gave me a confidence in this country, and I came to consider France a second home.

Yet, as a young girl straight out of the sheltered grammar-school ambiance of northern Scotland, I experienced racial and sexual discrimination with full force, which first began on my return to Paris from the private summer estate.

This time, I went to live with my patron's daughter and her family on Boulevard Mont St. Michel, looking after three young children while their parents' marriage was literally falling apart. In the meantime, I attended the Institute Catholique for French classes.

While I was living there in a small attic room, I became acquainted with my next-door neighbors—two brothers who came from the old French colonies, who were holding their sister captive in order to marry her off to a man of their choice. This situation blew my mind. I had never encountered such an awful idea like this before. At the same time, and against the backdrop of my charges' unhappy family life, I was viciously attacked by a madman who had followed me home to my little room above the family's apartment, after I had been out with a group of au pairs and nannies.

I hadn't heard him coming behind me, and when I opened my studio door, I found myself thrown down onto the floor violently. As he twisted my hair and pulled me up to my feet to attack me, the pain in my head caused me to pass out; hence, I have no memory of what happened. I didn't have the nerve to tell the family who employed me; so instead of getting help and counselling, I resigned my position and left rapidly to get away from the attacker who kept coming back to try and find me.

As a result of seeking other employment, I went to work for a wealthy Moroccan family with a little girl named Emmanuelle who lived opposite the Moulin Rogue in the Red Light district of Paris. I had moved, quite literally, from the rich zone to the poor zone in more ways than one.

This was such a weird world—a district that housed both the sex industry and the everyday normal businesses of life, such as supermarkets, offices, department stores, and schools. This area was then, and is even more so today, an area that is heavily inhabited by the colonial French citizens. To say the least, it was a highly colorful area for a young Scottish girl from a religious family.

At this time, I lived in a large, spacious, high-ceiling family...a view of this huge, white, domed church—*Basilique du Sacré-Coeur*, the

Sacred Heart Basilica, perched on top of one of Paris's hills, in the Montmartre artist quarter of Paris where Toulouse Lautrec, Vincent Van Gogh, and the Impressionist artists had lived during the 1800s. I knew as I looked at the contrast between this towering church above me and the streets below me that I was seeing a Dante vision of heaven and hell. The question for me, though, was—"Which one was which?" My aversion to religion of all denominations was by this time becoming very ingrained, and I saw no difference between the selling of sex on one hand, and the selling of indulgences on the other.

On another day, the reality of the sex workers took on a real face. One of the prostitutes, whose "patch" was next to my front door, stopped me to check me out. She was a tall lanky woman who wore an obvious wig perched on top of her head. Approaching me, she croaked, "Qu'est ce tu fais ici?" ("What are you doing here?") in a deep guttural Parisian accent. I was so scared that I squeaked back, "Je suis une jeune fille au pair ecossaise." ("I'm a young Scottish au pair/nanny.") When she heard my response, she nodded sagely, confirming I was no threat to her or her patch. After that encounter, I was looked after by all the "girls of the street" as well as by the police who escorted me from the metro entrance to my doorway.

Yet I never felt safe there. My attacker was still on my mind; in addition, being observed by a pimp while taking my young charge to school one day didn't help the situation. When I finally left Paris to return to live with my parents in Amsterdam, there was a real sense of relief to leave that part of the city behind me.

Now, as I prepared to drive across France to Germany, I was actually feeling quite in charge of my situation. I speak French, and I understand the French and their ways, so I considered this journey as no huge undertaking. Yet although I had been a tour guide in France and have lived in France on several other occasions, this was my first forage into Europe as a Gospel preaching, on-fire-for-Jesus, tongue-speaking, radical Pentecostal Christian! And guess what! The enemy was not standing with open arms when I got to Calais. How strange!

I can laugh now, but it was a tough experience. This was the next step up, which God took me to, in order to teach me how to stand with more strength. I had booked into two very nice "bijoux" hotels as a treat before starting my classes at the Bible seminary, and it was there that I encountered what was to become almost normal for me over the next few years.

I had been getting used to demonic disturbances, but now things got really personal. Wrestling with demons is not the most pleasant of experiences, but that is what started to happen. I experienced invisible things jumping on the bed, trying to strangle me, sticking their faces in mine—and yes, when God allows it—seeing into the spiritual realm—and no, you don't really want to. Demons are ugly; some of them look like hedgehogs with squished faces. And I could continue to describe others; but I want my focus here to be on Jesus and the knowledge that all demons will burn forever in the lake of fire when Jesus returns—straight Scripture from the Book of Revelation.

The first hotel I stayed at was so pretty and quaint, completely rural French. The food was haute cuisine and the hoteliers friendly and warm. Speaking French again was a delight, and I settled down to sleep that night quite relaxed for someone on the first leg of the journey to a mountaintop. Sometime in the middle of the night, though, I had a rude awakening, which measured a high ten on the scale of weirdness. Literally, something jumped on me! Okay, something like this happened once before in Scotland. But now, this was France, and this "thing" wouldn't go away. I turned over after explaining to any listening demons about the name of Jesus and the lake of fire and went back to sleep again, only to be awakened again and again.

The next day I moved on from this interesting idyllic tourist trap, feeling somewhat chagrined but looking forward to the rest of my journey. Later that day, I stopped in the mountains close to Strasbourg for a two-day layover of rest and relaxation. Upon arriving at the lovely hotel set amidst these foothills of middle France, I had the real pleasure of meeting a delightful Canadian couple who asked me what I was doing. So…I told them. They listened to my "undiluted" testimony, and we discussed their need to know Jesus, which changed their lives.

However, the next two nights gave me complete insight into French witchcraft at its nastiest. The Holy Spirit did not spare any detail of what the dark side is in this country. He showed me exactly what I had been living alongside for years before Jesus came to rescue me. When I left, I was no longer under any impression that there was any friendly ground for Christians on fire for Jesus—there was none whatsoever. I have also realized that Europe is one of the darkest places where a born-again Christian can live.

It had taken a few days to meander across France, travelling south of Paris, and finally, I came to the bottom of the last mountain. And what a wonderful surprise! When I lived in Turin, I had become used to travelling the hairpin bends and amazingly narrow roads of the Italian Alps, and as I started the climb up this mountain in the jeep, I was treated once again to challenging hairpin bends galore! It was great—real driving!

When I had visited the seminary the year before, I had flown into Stuttgart Airport. That particular drive from the airport does not indicate that you are approaching a mountaintop; whereas, from the French side, it is simply amazing. It seemed like that little road went on and on, and laughing all the way up, I exclaimed, "God, what are You doing to me? Why didn't You tell me?" What an amazing God we have! And then, this first journey to the seminary at Kniebis was finally completed.

As I arrived, I was welcomed by one of the students whom I had previously met at the week's counselling course. Christian opened the door, grinned at me, and said, "I knew you were coming back!" Just for saying that, I insisted that he help carry all my boxes up to my new room in the Bible school—number 35. It is one of the largest rooms at the end of the corridor with its own bathroom/shower and the most fantastic view over the mountaintop landscape. Kniebis is literally on top of the mountain; therefore, you can't see any other mountains nearby. But what you can see on a clear day are the Swiss Alps four hundred kilometers away on the other side of Lake Constance. I was warmly welcomed by Gabbi and Maite, the house mothers, and I started to settle in. Again, this setting was the absolute opposite of Hogwarts! Light, airy—radiant and happy young students all dedicated to serving the Lord. Incredible! Welcome to the mountaintop!

Chapter 8

BACK-TO-SCHOOL SYNDROME

And you know that He was revealed that He might take away our sins, and in Him is no sin (1 John 3:5).

Have you ever felt like you were in the right place at the right time, but you didn't quite know how you got there? This is how I felt when I first came to the European Theological Seminary (ETS for short). Upon completion of orientation week, during which we were introduced to each other and learned the rules and regulations of the school, classes started and the shock of community living really made an impact!

Still today, most of the students live in the seminary where there are over 30 rooms—doubles and singles, in addition to two apartments for on-campus staff. We all had to help with general housework during what is called the "work hour." This is a time after lunch and before the afternoon classes began. The students are divided into teams depending upon their abilities and depending upon what the house mothers need help with. So, at my own request, I spent my first year as a team leader for one of the kitchen teams.

The chef is a very interesting and very capable German ex-drug addict, with heavy metal, hard rock tattoos, who wears the typical chef's hat and clothes. Jesus saved him out of the pit years ago and has put him in charge of feeding His hungry Bible school students, which is a formidable task! In exchange, Joachim (who is married to a Jewish and who now has eight children) is paid and is provided with a work team to clean the kitchen and restaurant. Anyone who needs to learn about serving and servanthood discipline is assigned to work under Joachim! Because we both came from a druggie past, we were always having a laugh. This chef helped keep me on the "straight and narrow" of kingdom living.

The first year was an amazingly wonderful but difficult one for me. To begin with, getting back into a school atmosphere of study and student participation was painful! But the prayer life of the seminary was wonderful, and has become even better with even more ardent students being brought into the school by God. So the transition, though challenging at times, was endurable. You see, God had very kindly and faithfully given to me what I had requested of Him when I first started reading the Bible in Scotland. While reading through the Psalms, I came across Psalm 113:9: "He causes the barren to dwell in the house as a joyful mother of sons. Praise Jehovah!" My ex-husband and I had been unable to have children, so when I found this verse while living with my twin sister, I lifted the Bible up into the air and said to God, "Look!" God obviously did look and acted on my request! However, I don't think I imagined, when I pointed out this Psalm to our God that He would give me 80-plus young people to be loved by. But then, God doesn't do things half-heartedly, and His abundance is overflowing!

The other little detail here is that I had always wanted to live on top of a mountain in my pre-Jesus life; God also answered that desire as well.

The seminary curriculum starts in October and is framed by worship and prayer. A large number of students are worship and youth leaders "in the making," so there is always lots of noise and music everywhere. There are American missionary lecturers as well as British and German lecturers; consequently, lessons are bilingual.

Students come from Germany, Eastern and Western Europe, and other parts of the world; so, culture shock is definitely part of the learning process, which is good training for many of the young people who are missions-oriented.

I wasn't the only "more mature" student at the seminary. As part of their policy, the faculty recruits a few older students, and usually, there are mature African students sent to upgrade their theological degrees. These gentlemen are often overseers or bishops, who add a further interesting mix in this small community. One of these was Christopher who was in his second year of study when I arrived. He had left his family behind in Kenya to become equipped for the ministry of God, and his participation at early morning prayers and at devotions was so encouraging.

The first few months just whizzed past between lessons starting at eight o'clock in the morning and great music and prayer meetings every evening at nine o'clock, to finish off the day. December arrived quickly, and we started to get ready to go home for Christmas. Unfortunately, though, our brother from Kenya hadn't been given any funds to go home, and he was obviously missing his family. So, our president and his wife, Paul and Gabbi, decided to do something really special for him.

There was a large Christmas party planned with family and friends invited; everyone dressed up nicely and Joachim cooked us a wonderful Christmas dinner. Just before these Christmas festivities commenced, we had our last devotional service, which was scheduled twice a week when the worship team led the students in singing praise songs and someone gave a short message.

On this particular day, it was Peter's turn, from Uganda, to deliver the message. As he did so, Paul and Gabbi, along with the help of some of the students, started to trundle in a huge trolley holding a massive box wrapped in Christmas paper! As they pushed it into the chapel, Paul started to exclaim loudly, "My goodness, what have we got here!"

Christopher had been sitting, looking a bit downcast during this devotion time; and when he looked up, it was without any interest whatsoever. Only a few of us, including myself, knew what was happening but tried not to react to this incredible sight. As Paul passed by Christopher, he said, "There's a name on the parcel..." and then the trolley was positioned right at the front of the chapel. With a straight face, Paul continued, "Why, Brother Christopher...it's for you! It's got your name on it!"

At that point, some of us were holding onto our chairs to try to contain the excitement. Then, Christopher, who is only about five feet tall, walked up to the gift towering over him. Paul gave him a pair of scissors and directed him to start cutting at the front of the parcel where a huge heart had been drawn. As he started to cut, he peeked through the paper; and what did he see? All of the sudden, he stopped cutting and had to lean against the structure for a moment. By this time, students were clapping and singing and jumping up and down. Most had realized that this was a very special Christmas present, and within a few more moments, Christopher's wife, Rebecca, emerged from within the package! The two of them just stood there looking at each other—talk about a Christmas present! This is just one of the typical things that happened at this place. When you live for the love of Jesus, then the love of Jesus will shine through no matter what!

After the holidays, I started to settle into the routine and rhythm of the seminary, and God started His wonderful work on me. What I first learned was that when we come to know Jesus, then we can come to know His Father. As Jesus says in John 14:7, to know Him is to know the Father. Sometimes it's difficult to get to know Jesus, especially if we haven't had a brother or if we've had a poor relationship with a brother or brothers. But the Holy Spirit helps us to overcome these obstacles. For myself, the Holy Spirit led me to know Him and then the Father. It was not difficult because I had had a wonderful relationship with my own earthly dad, which did not interfere with how I could view God as a father figure.

However, my religious view of God was a different matter. From this point, I considered Him an angry, wrathful, nonhuman entity. You see, I hadn't realized that God actually wanted to know me! The world and religion teaches that if there is a God, then He is so big and too awesome to take any interest in us, and especially little ole me! What would God want to know me for? This was my modern, evolutionary, humanist mind-set. I even actually believed, totally and completely, that I evolved from the ape family.

Recently, I heard a reference to the theory of evolution that makes more sense to me than any complicated DNA chain—if we have evolved from monkeys, then why do monkeys still exist? Touché!

During the '80s and '90s when I had studied with the Open University and earned my BA in history, I was able to deal clinically and disinterestedly with the early history of man during the Renaissance and Reformation periods in relation to God. Michelangelo's iconic painting of God on the Sistine Chapel's ceiling made no sense to me whatsoever. Its depiction, when explained rationally, in light of symbolic motifs rooted in Italian art traditions, made more sense. But I wasn't looking at the figure of God; I was looking at the history behind the painting.

When my studies moved into the modern and postmodern eras, I was more able to connect with the lack of a god, any god, as I concentrated on the advancement of mankind's technologies and building successes. My studies into the existentialism of Jean Paul Sartre reinforced my own disbelief in a god, whether wrathful or caring, as I centered on man's pivotal position as the savior of mankind. And in the mind-set of the space industry, there was and still is the belief that mankind has to save mankind by removing a portion of the population from this planet before we totally run out of the earth's resources. This is the most insidious of all the lies of the world, which I came out of. Thinking I was related to a monkey was bad enough, but looking at a future of space colonization, in the light of Jesus, was appalling.

These teachings or indoctrinations, including Darwinism and humanism, had to be dismantled from my mind-set. I had been taught for years of the superiority of man over the world, so my worldview did not and could not accept a kind, loving, just, and righteous God. And then to realize the truth that this God wanted a relationship with me was just incredible!

This reality became even more personal as I was loved and accepted by the young people I was studying with. There was no question in these young people…had been "called." They all have incredible stories of how God grabbed their attention and drew them to Him and brought them to the seminary. In amongst the interesting mixture of young people were ex-satanists, ex-druggies, and normal everyday young people from various Protestant denominations. God "called" each one of them, including me, to come and discover more about Him. And what a crew!

Don't get me wrong—this wasn't always easy. Living in a remote village away from the sophistication of big city life was often not enjoyable; but it certainly helped to keep your mind focused, especially when the snow started to fall and didn't stop! By January, we had so much snow that the guys had constructed their own igloo in the parking lot, and some of the hardier (or crazier) ones were sleeping in it overnight. I declined the offer! There was so much snow, in fact, that at one point it got scary. Our work teams turned into snow detail teams to keep the parking areas free for us and the visitors!

And in between all of this, I was struggling with old issues—things like social drinking, which had been a part of my culture and which came as part-and-parcel of helping to run the local pub in my English village. This seminary had a no-alcohol policy, and so, Friday nights, which had once been such a pleasurable, social evening for me, could be horrendous. Many of the young people would go out and I would be left alone, babysitting the Bible seminary. On those nights, I had to dig deep with God to persevere, and I really struggled. Sometimes I had to go away for a weekend to clear my head from the extreme pressures forced on an ex-drinker by the enemy.

I realize that God hasn't got a problem with drinking alcohol in moderation. But if a person has struggled with an alcohol problem, or with any addiction, the best thing to do is to give it over to God and ask Him to take the addiction away.

But I didn't want to give this one habit up. I liked my glass of wine with a nice meal. It was the next glass or two that became the challenge, however. Yet I still hung onto the idea that I could overcome this problem by myself. I chuckle now, but oh, it was not a good idea to think that I was strong enough to conquer this battle on my own. God is the one who has the answer; still, He will wait for us to try to solve the situation ourselves before we finally come to Him and say, "Okay. What do You suggest?" In the meantime, I wrestled with God as well as with the enemy in this time of learning the hard way. The answer to this dilemma finally came when I was in my third year at the seminary but no longer living on campus. (More about that later.)

I now know that these types of issues must first be settled and dealt with by Jesus before we can stand firm for Him. But still, as a hardheaded human, I had to first try to do everything my own way rather than go to the One Person who could provide the solution.

It says in the Operating Manual, under First John 3:5, "And you know that He was revealed that He might take away our sins, and in Him is no sin." But what does this mean? To me it means that a person who comes from a lifestyle of addictions can go to Jesus, and He will literally help us to deal with all our problems. It's not a case that He *might* help, but that He *will* help. I learned that Jesus was there to help me with all my problems and that He could set me completely free—even from the sin problems such as alcoholism, drug addiction, and depression, leading to drug overdose, suicide, and other self-abusing actions. There's one catch though—you've got to know Jesus.

All those lonely Friday nights at the seminary taught me a great lesson—I didn't need to tell God how big my problems are, but I could certainly tell my problems how big my God is. Touché!

Chapter 9

AN EMPTY PLACE IN HELL

Stand fast in this way in the Lord, beloved ones (Philippians 4:1b).

I found myself very busy—studying, praying, working, eating, socializing—school days were simply flying by. And life on the surface seemed to be fine. But in reality, everything was not okay. During the night, I was still suffering from the most horrendous attacks by the enemy.

You might ask, and people did ask, "What!? You're still getting attacked in a...Bible school?" Oh yes, the enemy hates our Bible schools, and these schools need lots of prayer and prayer coverings. In fact, there was and continues to be an active witches coven in a local nearby village that preys on and prays against the seminary. Witch training schools like Hogwarts reportedly exist.

A missionary friend in Eastern Europe visited a castle as part of a tourist group, where he saw a group of children wearing wizard and witch clothing, being hastily hurried out of the basement kitchen and leaving their food behind on wooden platters as they departed. When my friend inquired as to what was going on, he was told that there was a "Harry Potter Weekend" being held. Parents who send their children to these types of summer camps at these schools, thinking that it's "just a bit of fun" should beware.

So, although I was busy and actively participating in the school curriculum during the day, by night it was a different story—an all-out assault by the enemy. I would go to bed, commit myself into the hands of the Lord, and soon be asleep; and then sometime during the early hours of the morning, "something" would jump on me!

Only a few teachers and a handful of students actually knew what was happening. At one point, the situation became so distressing that the president came to pray in my room. At that point, he inquired, somewhat hopefully, if it wasn't just the heating system causing disturbances in the air. I politely and carefully replied that I had been married to a thermal engineer for years and knew the difference between rising air and being physically weighed down during the night!

I now am aware that while some of the teachers had realized what was happening to me, they still didn't know what to do for me, and God didn't seem to be providing any answers. Others just didn't "do demons." Many of the students shied away from this area, and most of the faculty did not want to teach on it, claiming, quite correctly, that concentrating on the enemy takes our focus off Jesus. So, it became a question of finding the right balance.

On one particular occasion, one of the teachers' wives tried limiting the situation by suggesting that a cat was coming into my room; but there were no cats in the school. (And since when do cats try to strangle you?) Needless to say, it wasn't a pleasant situation. And it didn't make sense to anyone, including me.

Then one night, the Holy Spirit woke me up with a vision of two wizards incanting. I saw that they had written the word "spirit" on a blackboard between them, and while I was still trying to discern what this was all about, something hit me hard. Suddenly, I was thrust into the midst of a physical battle. I quickly realized that these two wizards had incanted up some obnoxious spirit aimed right at me. You can understand why I have now given up wizard films like *Harry Potter, Lord of the Rings,* and *The Wizard of Oz.* This subject doesn't make me laugh anymore.

The Holy Spirit showed me through these encounters that the devil hates his own human servants as well as Christians, which is why it is a good idea to pray for these people and forgive them. Asking Jesus to also save them annoys the hell out of satan! At another time, as I was praying in the seminary chapel, a phrase kept recurring in my mind—"Leave my people alone." Because we all are created in the image of God, I started to take hold of the fact that we need to stand even stronger against the enemy who wants to especially take out young Christians before they can mature. I, as a young Christian myself, was obviously seen as a potential threat, and unfortunately as such, was still unable to deal with these types of attacks.

I eventually discovered that as well as learning to stand, we must also learn to stand *together,* for it is even better than standing alone. In Matthew 18:20, Jesus says, "For where two or three are gathered together in My name, there I am in their midst." There is a power in spiritual unity, just as in any kind of physical togetherness. The sniper can pick us off one at a time when we are alone; but when we stand together, it is much more difficult to attack a stronger force. Moreover, offensively, several pairs of spiritual eyes, rather than one, can more easily spot the sniper, thereby putting him out of action more quickly.

In the meantime, I still wasn't managing to put God's power into practice. And that is what spiritual authority is all about—practice. This is why schools like Ellel are important; they are an absolute necessity if we really believe we are living in the last days. Just as we need to practice how to learn to play the piano, or to cook, or to drive, we also need to practice how to have our authority over the kingdom of darkness.

Finally, the Holy Spirit brought me to a place where I realized just how dire our situation is, which activated and motivated me to do some serious practice. Alongside the practicing of our authority is also living what is called a holy life. This doesn't mean being a "goody-two-shoes," as I had been brought up to understand. There is nothing mankind can do to earn salvation; we are saved only by Jesus Christ. Yet as a Christian, I still hadn't quite reached that understanding, and I was trying to be a "good person" while wrestling with areas such as sexuality and the ongoing desires of worldly living. The reality of this process was brought home to me very clearly one night when I had returned to England to visit my parents in the first year at Christmastime.

Before returning, I had bought myself a beautiful gold ring in the local town of Freudenstadt and had the name "Jesus" inscribed on it—not on the inside, but on the outside. I had worn a wedding band for a long time, and I missed having a ring on my finger. There had also been an unfortunate incident that brought attention to my single, mature, divorced status. Unfortunately, my friendly nature had been misunderstood; and consequently, I needed to take a serious look at my behavior. You can't change other people, but you can change yourself; so, that is what I set out to do.

I had bought a special ring—a wedding band ring to wear on my left hand, as a declaration and as a statement of my serious intention toward Jesus. Well, that ring caused all havoc from hell to break loose. It became very obvious that the devil doesn't like this sort of thing, and the fight became quite intense—so intense that the Holy Spirit had to help me understand the commitment I was making to Jesus by wearing this ring.

One night, while my parents slept soundly in their beds at their home in Bournemouth, my little room with a single bed turned into another reality. The Holy Spirit took me in the spirit, into the upper levels of sheol and showed me exactly where my spot had been. Until you have been in hell you might not really understand or know why we need to proclaim the Gospel.

The Holy Spirit flew me down a long reddish-black tunnel that emerged into a huge cavern. As I looked down upon the countless shrouded heads, I felt a fear and a dread that I never ever want to experience again. Lines and lines upon lines of people were beneath me as I was taken through this vast, dimly lit cavern. The dark red gloom I now know was the color of the blood of Jesus, which is what I had been looking through on this awful visitation. And finally, the Holy Spirit brought me to an empty space in one of the lines of people against a wall, of which I suddenly knew that it had been *my place.*

For an awful second, I thought that I was going to be left there. I even felt the presence of the Holy Spirit departing for just a moment. I had been seeing this vision with my eyes closed in my darkened room. So, in order to stop the vision, I opened my eyes, but found myself still in that place. My heart nearly stopped with the absolute fear of being left there.

Then the Holy Spirit's presence returned, and I was led back out of the massive cavern, back over the heads of all those people, those souls, and back up the tunnel. I don't know why I couldn't just open my eyes and walk away from that place. All I know is that the Holy Spirit chose to fly me back out of there before I came back to the reality of this world. Then, I was left laying on my bed with no strength and no feeling at all.

Complete desolation came over me at the knowledge of where I had just been, and what it really meant hit me fully within my inner being. Hell is the destination for all mankind unless you know and belong to Jesus. And once you have been in hell you can never be the same again—ever. Being holy actually means "set apart" in Greek, which is the original language in which the New Testament was written. It does not mean "being good." Rather, being "set apart" means just that—being taken out of the mass of mankind who are blind to the reality of their final destination, and allowing Jesus, His Father, and His Holy Spirit to deliver you from the blindness and self-deception of your own real reality. The existence of hell is so grim that I can't even try to explain it. And after this experience, my whole perception of life changed. The process of learning to overcome all obstacles in order to stand my ground, as explained in Ephesians 6:13, now started to kick in.

I had experienced the meeting with Jesus in my cottage in England, and now, during my first year of seminary, I finally started to understand what Jesus had done for me. He had literally given His life for mine as an exchange. That place I had seen in hell would remain empty because I had crossed over from the ownership of the devil to the ownership of Jesus.

This concept of being owned, however, initially offended my human pride and independent personality. Yet, fortunately, I was delivered from the indoctrination of the world that teaches us that we belong to ourselves. Realizing the presence of hell takes away all world pride in man-made belief systems based upon philosophies that have no provable foundations. What is the point of "earthly wisdom," (which is what the word *philosophy* means in Greek), if you end up in hell?

I now returned to the seminary for the second part of the first year with an added knowledge, but one which I did not feel at liberty yet to share. I realized that what I was experiencing wasn't always appreciated by my own Christian family. These experiences were often seen as intimidating and fearful, even by the students in the seminary. Having been an atheist, I knew how important it is not to isolate or intimidate non-believers, and in the same vein, believers as well. I understood from my own perspective that to "win people for Christ" has many different meanings and approaches. I can personally testify to this, clearly remembering how I would scream abuse at my twin sister when she tried to tell me about her Jesus. This abuse was something she had also earlier experienced from me and our older brother after her own radical conversion encounter in her early 20s.

During lunch one day at the Amsterdam manse, she had been testifying to our family about an encounter she had had with Jesus; and my brother and I started mocking her in front of our parents, ridiculing her and asking her where had she "found her Jesus." We were very cruel to her, sarcastically deriding her and saying she must have looked in a bin, and guess what—there was Jesus! Interestingly, neither of my parents interrupted this flow of angry dismissal at their table.

Yet it was my sister's prayers that were the initial preparation for bringing me out of the kingdom of satan and into the Kingdom of God. Prayer is the powerful spoken word that connects with Jesus in the spiritual realm and starts the process of a person's salvation. My sister's prayers were heard by Jesus, and as Jesus tells us, her prayers would not return void. He dynamically answers all of them. All my experiences up until this time made me realize just how high a value Jesus places on each one of us, and just how hard satan fights for each one of us as well.

Meanwhile, during our evangelization class at this time, I, along with the other students, was learning how to testify and give a personal testimony, which is so important. I understood from my hell visit that Jesus had to come and rescue us, and the only way for Him to accomplish this was by giving up His life for us on the cross. This new life through the cross of Jesus was something I had never understood, but now the meaning was being revealed. The blood that Jesus had spilt for me represents the lifeline of truth that I, as a member of mankind, had severed with God for a false promise from satan. This brought the curse that has been and continues to be passed on through the unknowing generations. We are born condemned, and we don't even know it! We need to always remember the following Reinhard Bonnke war cry that a prayer warrior, by the name of Tina at the seminary, posted above her door:

Plunder hell to populate Heaven.

The unknown, eternal death knell of modern, sophisticated mankind was especially brought home to me one night as I was getting ready to fall asleep. I suddenly heard the voice of a well-to-do young man saying loudly and indignantly, "I have my rights." This voice was then abruptly cut off; but I knew instantly that what I had heard was a person insisting that he, even on being taken into the depths of eternal hell—that he still had rights. I heard this voice during the same time I had been wrestling with my belief that I also "had rights."

Subsequently, the Holy Spirit revealed to me that we have no rights. We have never had rights and we never will have rights—that is the lie of the devil. The eternal truth is, we either belong to God, or we belong to satan—one or the other. I have discovered, as a child of God, that as I grow in God I know that He has given me the right to either have a relationship with Him or not. This is called "free will," and God will not go against our free will. If we don't want to know Him, then we can say no. But we then also need to realize that even so, we still don't belong to ourselves, but to the devil. Hence, our sophisticated belief system, which denies the devil's existence, damns us to hell.

So as I lay in my bed at the Bible seminary, being attacked during the night, getting up and proceeding through the day's activities with hardly any sleep for the first two years, I came to realize I was in the midst of an intense battle zone. But in that atmosphere of war, God was proving me. He was testing me and thereby increasing my tenacity as a Christian. My desire to know Jesus was increasing; and the Potter, our Creator, described by Isaiah in the Old Testament, was molding me into shape.

Chapter 10

REMOLDED

But now, O Jehovah, You are our Father; we are the clay, and You are our Former; and we all are the work of Your hand (Isaiah 64:8).

During my first year at Kniebis, I joined the seminary church called CrossRoads International Church and became part of a team, a cellgroup outreach ministering to African asylum seekers. At this time of my life, I was in the process of being remolded and reeducated by God—what the apostle Paul calls "renewing the mind"—literally being reoriented from the things of the world kingdom into the things of the Kingdom of God.

Earlier in my life, I had been a consular clerk in Amsterdam and in Antwerp, where the attitude toward people applying for visas could be very negative and pessimistic. Anyone seeking entrance into Great Britain was often considered a possible undercover asylum seeker or terrorist; and it was common opinion that the intensions of immigrants be disclosed by whatever means were available.

Normally, the questioning took place in an interview process where, on one occasion, my colleague found a stack of bank notes hidden in a passport handed through the opening of a bullet-proof glass of the interviewing box. Because of attempts like these, it's not surprising that visa officers had become cynical and arrogant in their attitude toward applicants.

Nevertheless, I thought it perfect that God had not only placed me in an asylum seekers' cellgroup, but that He had also given me a heart for these people. God changed the faces of the asylum seekers from non-descript and unimportant to real live people with oppressive needs and significant problems.

Suddenly, these people became my concern. They became my responsibility; they became my family not only in Christ but as real human beings who needed to be loved and encouraged. But what really grieved me was how these people were being treated by the authorities, which in turn forced them to make poor choices in a hostile world.

Many of the women in our group had applied for asylum on humanitarian grounds to escape their country's practice of female circumcision. I eventually took them, with their babies, to visit lawyers several hundred kilometers away in Heidelberg.

These women were so desperate to stay in Germany that they would go to such measures as to become pregnant by men with German residential papers so that they could claim the right to also stay in Germany along with their babies, who were considered legal German citizens. This "loophole" encouraged these women to have illegitimate children. It did not matter if they were married or not to the fathers of their children.

Their predicament continues to break my heart. The housing given to these people is horrendous. One of the places where these particular women resided was an old, damp, cold, stinking meat factory. The authorities deliberately gave them the worst places to live in order to discourage them from submitting applications for residence.

I continued to do whatever I could to help them, and on one particular occasion, I decided to take them on a picnic—a day out. And never have I ever experienced such a day as that one!

I was driving one of our seminary vans, transporting eight African women and their babies in the middle of the Black Forest of Germany, when one of the women, a strong-minded leader of the group, explained to me that she didn't like forests. To her people back home, forests represented dark and ill-omened places where witch doctors and spirits rule.

I felt badly, for I had wanted to take them somewhere nice for the day; and I thought the Black Forest along with its picturesque villages and charming spa towns, where you often find unique hotels and facilities with special waters and supposedly therapeutic healing sources, would make for a perfect outing.

As I realized the mistake I was making by escorting this group into places considered threatening and haunting, I also realized the immense difference between our cultures. These people not only believe in evil spirits; they also understand how much these spirits desire to mutilate and kill them before they can come to Jesus. The people are confused with a mixture of religious ritualism and voodoo superstitions. The very act of female circumcision demonstrates the hatred of satan toward mankind and especially toward the woman—the bearer of children. Satan delights in nothing more than the mutilation of God's creation. (With regard to this topic, you can read a very interesting story in the Book of First Kings. When Elijah challenged the priests of Baal on top of Mount Carmel, the priests spent the entire day worshipping their gods, committing acts of self-mutilation—see First Kings 18:28—and still failed to win the challenge.)

One night, after having visited with "my ladies," as I referred to them, and laying my hands upon them, I went to bed and was startled awake by the sound of jungle drums in the distance. This was the first time I had ever encountered such sound effects, and it made me more determined to continue helping them in any way possible.

Meanwhile, I continued with my studies, and the nighttime visitations continued as well. Sometimes I would come to class so exhausted that I didn't know, and I still don't know, how I managed to get through it. Months passed, and exams came with all the added stress and strain; yet I somehow was able to cope because I knew God was watching over me. He was aware of all my circumstances, and provided me with Scriptures to encourage and strengthen me.

As the end of that first year approached, I had to make a serious decision about the future. Would I continue studying at the seminary for another two years, or accept a Foundation Course diploma and return to Scotland to take up my place at Aberdeen University in order to train to be a history teacher? That place had been held open for me for one year; and to choose not to return to Scotland would mean losing my position as a student and subsequently submitting a reapplication if things didn't work out at the German seminary.

This was no easy decision. I had not been able to receive a financial grant in order to study in Germany even though I was in the European Community; thus, I had been paying all my own fees and living costs there. In addition, I also had to consider my health. I knew I wasn't getting any younger and there was an issue of scheduling an operation for an old physical problem. But even in the face of the financial cost as well as the social cost, I decided to stay on.

Being totally honest, the thought of returning to the wet, cold, granite-stoned city of Aberdeen didn't really appeal to me, especially while looking out over the woodland landscape of the Black Forest and its surrounding countryside. God knew this, of course; apparently, the only person who didn't quickly realize what I should do was me.

When I finally determined to stay on, I told one young lady, who had been a missionary in South America, about my decision. She looked at me in amazement and said, "But of course you are staying. There wasn't any other question, was there?" Touché.

Immediately after making my decision, I climbed up the stairs to my room on the third floor in between classes to fetch something. And when I walked into my room, I found a long curved rainbow, nearly three feet long, majestically displayed on my sloped attic ceiling in radiant, beautiful colors! Talk about being stopped in your tracks!

Even though I was in a hurry between classes, I took a moment to gaze at it with amazement. Fortunately, I thought to pick up my camera, took some pictures, and then quickly departed for the next class. Because we were approaching the end of the term, which brought with it a hurried anticipation, as students were packing their belongings, organizing their rooms, and cleaning the seminary in preparation for the summer courses, I forgot all about the pictures.

Most students were preparing to leave to take up their summer practicum placements, and mine was to be at the New Testament Church of God in Southampton, southern England, close to my parents. At this point, I still did not realize just how real the relationship with the Holy Spirit was about to become, and I drove off to England.

You could describe the next stage of my "molding" process as challenging and intensive. God doesn't do things partially or only to a certain degree, and my choice (or was it God's choice?) of practicum turned out to be quite demanding.

At this time, I still did not understand that the money I had received from the divorce proceedings was actually God's provision for me. When my ex-husband bought my share of our home, this money was to pay for the first part of my new life—in this case, seminary fees and expenses. It wasn't possible for me to buy him out because, quite honestly, I didn't have a job that could support the kind of mortgage our expensive village cottage required. My job had been to take care of my husband, so I hadn't had much choice in the decision behind the offer to buy me out of our 20-year home. However, this God-given provision proved to be a blessing so that I would be able to travel to various places in the first few years, until I discovered the financial blessings that only God can give.

Christians who are financially secure are a serious threat to the enemy; they pay for kingdom business to be accomplished through honoring God with tithing and giving donations. I personally believe that when God sees we are able to be responsible with His finances, then He will trust us with more.

As a young and susceptible Christian, I was about to learn that if you do have any money, the devil will try to steal it from you! God was showing me that giving is good, but I was to make sure that it was God who was directing me to give. Wisdom is needed, especially when there are many wolves posing as Christians. I was taught Jesus' instructions to be alert for predators, both believers and nonbelievers, who dress up as kind and pious people. Jesus says in Matthew 10:16: "Behold, I send you out as sheep in the midst of wolves. Therefore be as *wise* as serpents and as *harmless* as doves." I would personally meet with one of these wolves later in the summertime. I did use wisdom, but unfortunately, it was in hindsight!

Jesus used the words *wise* and *harmless,* giving us…In the Greek, other interpretations for these two words include "thoughtful" or "discreet" for the word *wise,* and "innocent" or "simple" for the word *harmless.*

I learned that we, the people of God, need to be cautious while remaining "simple" in our ways when dealing with the world. The word *simple* does not mean "stupid," as I had been brought up to understand; rather it means "to be childlike or innocent," as Jesus described in Matthew when He stated to allow the children to come to Him "for of such is the kingdom of Heaven" (see Matt. 19:14).

Speaking of word descriptions, when I was young, words that I had heard used to describe Jesus included "meek and mild." This picture of Jesus, however, gave me an impression of weakness rather than strength. This is a sad reflection of my childhood and of growing up in a Scottish countryside parish in rural Aberdeenshire, where my family was literally as poor as church mice. Jesus did not come across as a strong person in my upbringing; in fact, in those days, I don't remember hearing much about Jesus at all.

My parents were of mixed British heritage; my mother, Welsh-English, and my father, Welsh-Scottish. They had arrived in Scotland so that my dad could complete his theology degree in Glasgow in order to join the Church of Scotland, drawn by the radical social preaching of Reverend George McCloud in the late 1950s. There, they would settle down and raise a family.

This life was interrupted when I was three years old, when dad joined the Royal Air Force as a chaplain, and we went, as a family, to live in Changai, Singapore at the RAF base for three years. Dad then decided to leave the force, and we returned to Scotland where he had been invited to minister. This time, we went to a small rural village called Fyvie, tucked away in the heart of Aberdeenshire. There we lived in a huge, old, Victorian parish manse with servants' quarters and a wonderful dark, damp cellar where we played hide-and-seek. But we froze in the winters when we couldn't afford the oil central heating. I remember being resentful because we were so poor and the village people were so mean to us. Mum had to go to what was called "jumble sales" to buy our clothes, and there was never enough to go around. And as a kid, I would negatively wonder, *What sort of God would leave us so poor?*

By the time I was 13, when we moved to Aberdeen for dad to take up the position as minister to the Church of West St. Nicholas, I had no interest in this poor Jesus. I had never seen or been privileged to receive any of His riches, and even though we moved to a manse that was located on one of the poshest streets in Aberdeen, things just got worse.

There had been no double glazing of the houses' windows although there was a constant freezing northeast wind that would sweep through the city. Moreover, the church wouldn't pay for such work to be done. So, dad had to put up thick plastic sheets on the inside of the windows to try keep in what little heat we did have! Can you imagine how excruciatingly embarrassing this was for young teenagers walking up a road full of Bentleys, Jaguars, and Range Rovers, to come to our house with its poor little car outside the gate and thick plastic sheets on the inside of the windows? What would you have thought?

So, needless to say, this resentment still remained toward "God's people" and had to be dealt with. The starting point came as I drove over to Britain in an expensive 4x4 jeep, a remnant of my married life. I was to begin a practicum in one of the poorest areas of Southampton, full of the most interesting of characters I had yet met on this new journey of life with Jesus.

At this point, I still didn't have the simple understanding of how uncomplicated it really is to be a child of God while also being a good steward of His provision. But I was about to find out, and it would soon become very apparent that I would need all of God's wisdom to hold onto what God had given me!

I had chosen Southampton as my practicum placement for two reasons. First, when I met the dynamic and charismatic overseer for the New Testament Church of God at the seminary, he had accepted my request to serve in one of his churches. This church was founded by the Afro-Caribbean immigrants who were invited to come to the British Isles in the 1960s and who then stayed on and made Britain their second home.

Second, I also wanted to be close to my parents because my father was dying of liver cancer, although we still didn't know how serious it was at that time.

I arrived just in time for the "Revival Week of Worship" to begin, which their reverend had asked me to come and be a part of. I had had no rest in between the end of the semester and exams, and the start of this amazing time of ministry. I was kindly invited to stay with one of the women members who was and continues to be a leading light in that community. She showed me a Christian lifestyle that can only be described as beautifully holy in the middle of a secular world. The revival meetings also gave me another insight and perspective of what Pentecost is about for our mixed cultures.

Each day, the pastor, another woman preacher who had been invited from America, and I shared the giving of the message. It was quite a week! And we had revival! The Holy Spirit came in His power and spoke to us, through us, and with us. This was my first experience of being out in ministry without my fellow students, and I experienced some huge learning curves.

One instance was during a service where the new converts were receiving the baptism of the Holy Spirit. I was praying for one dear Catholic woman when the assistant woman pastor came past me and asked, "Is she filled?" I was totally perplexed. *Is she what?* And then I realized that she meant, "Has she received the baptism of the Holy Spirit?" I had been so busy praying I hadn't noticed that the lovely Holy Spirit had already taken up residence, and it was with much laughing and hugging that this woman was set free from the bondages of the old life. How wonderful.

We also had an "upper room" experience that left me stunned when the Holy Spirit came in full power. I had just given a message on authority to the women of the church in the large upstairs sitting room of the church hall when I heard the words in my head, "Discern this," and then the Holy Spirit fell. There is no other description for this visitation and manifestation of God's Holy Spirit! The women were singing and laughing; one was baptized in the Holy Spirit while others were being set free from many burdens. It was glorious!

I served with this church for six weeks while spending my free time with my parents and witnessing my dad's increasingly deteriorating health. We still didn't know the extent of the illness, and furthermore, a mistake had been made in prescribing Statins—a medicine to lower blood pressure, the side effects of which were adversely affecting my father's overall condition.

It was during one visit that he and I finally got to know each other as Christians. There was still his lack of understanding about the Holy Spirit, and the fact that the Holy Spirit and the gifts of the Holy Spirit are freely available for us today. But in any case, we were starting to talk the same talk and walk the same walk, which was a real blessing.

I went with him to the little Anglican churches he was ministering to in the beautiful low-lying valleys of southeast England, and I felt very proud to be his daughter. At this point, he could no longer walk without help; and in addition, he needed my assistance to dress in his vestments, which many ministers still wear in the traditional church. This was also a time of bridge building. My father's traditional Christian friends and congregation knew I was a fully blown Pentecostal Christian; and they wondered if I would be a threat to their faith and their worship styles.

When I had finished my practicum, I bundled dad and mum into my car, and we went off for what would be my dad's last trip to France where we ate his favorite shellfish meals and generally got along fine, considering his ill health and my mother's need for a rest as well.

It was on this last trip that God revealed to me what had turned me away from Jesus and away from my family's religion when I was younger. I learned what Jesus meant when He said, "My mother and My brothers are those who hear the Word of God and do it" (Luke 8:21). I encountered the spirit of religion, which replaces the truth of Jesus with the falseness of man-made religion and the falsehood of trying to please a God portrayed as wrathful and unjust. I saw the effects that satan had had on my parents' lives through this spirit of religion, which was ruining their last few years together as a minister and wife of the traditional church. The truth is, where the Spirit of the Lord is there is freedom… but there was no freedom in my parents' lives.

It would be only a few months later that I would sit at the side of my father's sick bed in the hospital and lead him to Jesus Christ as his personal Savior and Lord. As I was sitting next to him, I felt led by the Holy Spirit to start reading the Book of John to him. When I came to the part where Jesus performed his first miracle of changing the water into wine, suddenly dad, who was moving in and out of consciousness, said, "Stop reading that—it's too strong." And then he relapsed into a semi-state of consciousness.

I was startled at his response; yet the Holy Spirit prompted me to get up, pour some water into a cup, consecrate it, and then prop dad up into a sitting position. When I did so, my dad became conscious and looked surprised; and I knew in that previous moment, he hadn't been himself. I then said to him, "Dad, *now* you are going to confess Jesus as your personal Lord and Savior." His eyes met mine, and I knew that he was aware and understood what was happening. He nodded weakly and tried to say the words, but they wouldn't come out. So I encouraged him, and after he spat, the words came out. He then spoke forgiveness toward all the people he had ever known. As he sank back into the pillows, I baptized him in the name of the Father, the Son, and the Holy Spirit.

My father had been a Bible-thumping, Gospel preacher for over 50 years, yet he had never known Jesus Christ. He knew the theology; he knew the doctrines; he knew the catechisms and the liturgy; he knew the church history; but he never knew Jesus personally.

One of the reasons I didn't want to become a Christian before Jesus spoke to me was because of "religious people." To me, religious people were misguided, crazy people who needed to dress up in strange clothing, stick their noses into other people's business, or looked for God in statues and incense and candles; others were busy trying to buy their way into Heaven. Now I know, with compassion, that these people are completely missing the focal point of Jesus and may end up in hell.

This was the spirit that had controlled my father's life even as he thumped the top of the pulpit as he preached "Jesus." This deception makes my own prior belief system of science fiction (intergalactic travel from planet to planet via a highway system of wormholes and connecting "beam-me-up-Scotty" transporters—Star Trek) look rather pathetic. At least I knew I was reading science fiction fantasy, but my dad was not only preaching a Jesus he didn't know, but was also being used, abused, and manipulated by the arch enemy. Beware of tradition, religion, and godly men dressed up as sheep but who are snarling ravenous wolves.

Chapter 11

TRICKERY IN TAIZE

Beware lest anyone rob you through philosophy and vain deceit, according to the tradition of men, according to the elements of the world, and not according to Christ (Colossians 2:8).

So what gives me the right to warn people about a religious spirit? Well, I've experienced firsthand the enemy's snares and traps, and I've made some mistakes. Fortunately, many times we learn more from the lessons that we fail than those where we succeed. This was one time where my lack of discernment was seriously challenged, yet consequently, I gained a wealth of understanding.

As I headed back to the seminary for the beginning of the second year, I had a week to spare. And it just "occurred" to me that on my way, I should visit a religious community located in the south of France, north of Lyon, called Taize.

My mother had mentioned this place in conversation a few times, and I had become aware that many Anglican friends of my parents, in ministry themselves, were spending time there to meditate and rest in order to find an "inner peace" with God. I myself, at this time, was wrestling with the dilemma of connecting different denominations and building bridges between them.

Pondering this subject, I set off on the journey to Macon via the port of Cherbourg. I knew that route extremely well from the many trips I had made with my husband, driving back and forth from Italy to our home in England. Therefore, I wasn't concerned about going solo. (However, I had obviously forgotten my journey across France on my way to the seminary!) This trip would turn out to be even more of an eye-opener! Yet I knew that I was not alone; and while musing to myself on the drive between worship songs, I told the Holy Spirit in a thought, *I will not be anxious anymore,* to which I received an audible reply, "Thank you." I was delightedly shocked to hear the Holy Spirit actually speak out loud. It doesn't happen too often for me!

On route, I stopped at the small village of Colombey-les-Deux-Eglise where the president of France during the Second World War, Charles de Gaulle, had been born, where he lived and died, and where the treaty was signed at the end of the Second World War. Up on a hill that overlooks the village is an amazing cross, called the Lorraine Cross, which has been built with a double cross bar, the smaller top bar representing the sign upon which the words were written, "Here is the King of the Jews."

As an ex-tour guide, I thought this was an interesting place to stop, and I found a small local pension (hotel) with the intention of being a tourist for a couple of days. This simple expectation soon disappeared, however, when during the night the resident demon, which obviously had no competition in that area, and obviously no other born-again Christians to attack, leaped on me, and kept leaping on me until morning came.

I was really concerned about this episode, as you can imagine; so I phoned my pastor's wife in Scotland for guidance. As we spoke about what had happened, she received a revelation from God, which she passed on to me—"Your bravado in the face of all the enemy attacks is removing you out from under God's covering." I had been busily telling the demons that I wasn't afraid of them because I was the daughter of God on high; but, in fact, I was afraid. And I wasn't handing this fear over to Jesus. I was lying, and satan was using that lie against me.

Although I was at first surprised by this message, upon reflection I realized that what I had been told was true. Instead of handing my problems over to Jesus and trusting in Him to protect me, I was attempting to fight the enemy with my own strength—which is impossible to do. This mistake, though simple, was costing me much.

This was, and continues to be an extremely important lesson for me to learn. The apostle Paul wrote in Romans, "But put on the Lord Jesus Christ" (Rom. 13:14). The very literalistic interpretation of the Scriptures is breathtaking; we have to wear Jesus as our protection from the enemy. This was also the first time I realized the special importance of prayer support covering. I simply thought I was going off for a quiet week of relaxation; but even when I was just trying to be quiet and mind my own business, the demoniacs wouldn't leave me alone.

I wondered why it was that I had to phone my pastor's wife to receive God's message about my own blindness, but I have since realized that by phoning her, she was able to intercede for me, along with her husband, and provide me with a prayer covering that I didn't previously have. Since then, the Holy Spirit has shown me that when soldiers go into a war zone, they must proceed with backup if they are to win the battle. Likewise, we Christians must do the same. What I hadn't figured on was that by going to Taize, I wouldn't be enjoying an anticipated quiet rest. Yet this fact should have been obvious, especially because I was visiting a religious, ecumenical, syncretic, multicultural youth camp. I was obviously going somewhere the enemy didn't want me to go.

I think most of my life before Christ had been lived with a false sense of bravado, and it took me a while to understand that this feeling is a lie. But once I gave this self-deception of my own protection over to Jesus, I was subsequently able to hand over all my fears to

Him. I could then receive His protection. Calling on the name of Jesus always breaks these attacks; whereas, being self-reliant doesn't. And as I made my way to this religious community of spiritualism and mysticism, the attacks eased.

When I finally arrived amidst the rolling countryside of this rich wine-producing region of France, I found a beautiful small town next to the community of Taize itself and made myself comfortable in a local hotel.

Because I had been an international tour guide at one time, I cannot really express the pain which this journey and others like it continue to cause me. My tour-guide days had been before my Christian experience; now, I saw these well-known places with different eyes. As I passed by these little bijoux places, so quaint and pretty, I gravely realized that these people, of whom I had been one, were all headed for hell unless they knew Jesus. Coming into this religious community challenged my understanding of how God works. Yes, I believe that God meets with us wherever He wants to—even within that community. But there were other spirits there as well, causing confusion and distracting attention from the focal point of Christianity—Jesus.

Taize is run by an ecumenical community of brothers, both monks and contemplatives, who through prayer, silence, and fellowship, offer their way of life for young people to join in with each summer. The worship starts once the robed monks and brothers enter and sit down on prayer stools, which are located in a central aisle down the middle of the sanctuary. The altar is a huge stage swathed in orange sheets with hundreds of burning candles. The service centers on a Scripture being read in many different languages, followed by singing and chanting with a heavy influence of the iconic and Eastern Orthodox traditions. The youth camp itself attracts over fifty thousand young people each year, and the organizers are both Protestant and Catholic; but no Pentecostal evangelical groups such as Vineyard are represented as of yet. After the main holiday season, the retreat is opened up to older people, as it was when I attended.

At one of the worship times, I found myself sitting in this esoteric, orange-colored sanctuary carefully observing the people. Then when I closed my eyes, I received a vision of who I had just been looking at, except the people were covered with a black funeral cloth instead. The thought came to me—*Many of these people won't make it*. What did this mean? I believe that when man dresses up in religion, when man decorates and translates a simple belief system into something esoteric and exotic, then it is religion that becomes the focal point of worship and relationship, and not God. I believe this is why God wanted me to visit Taize—to see the contrast in denominational and ecumenical worship in relation to a future ministry that I would be part of before I left Europe.

It was at this place that I also met an interesting man, whose name was Ken. He had introduced himself to me as an aging Anglican priest/missionary from an African country, who had come to find a quiet place to meditate and…to commit suicide. I was appalled as he confided his purpose to me at the hotel where we were both staying.

During the next several days, we engaged in several serious talks about life along with its multitude of problems. I became very involved with him on a personal level, concerned and worried at his decision to abandon not only his wonderful missionary work, but to give up on God as well.

At one point, he showed me his professional documentation and fundraising publications that he had brought with him to try and bail out the ailing mission fund he had been managing. Eventually, I invited and escorted Ken back to the seminary with me after his attempted suicide at the French hotel.

He was made very comfortable and was welcomed at the seminary by both faculty and students alike. However, his behavior became even more strange, even after spending a month among Holy Spirit-filled, on-fire-for-Jesus people. Along with his personality, his appearance began to change as well, with his face looking snake-like.

The resident demons finally couldn't stand the pressure and were showing themselves visibly—not a pretty sight!

This is when God led me on an interesting road of discovery. From the time I first met him, I had felt uncomfortable and knew there was something wrong. But it took me nearly two months to unearth the truth, and only then with the final push by the Holy Spirit did I learn that the devil comes in many disguises!

Finally, one morning, our president's wife couldn't stand it any longer and she pleaded with God to reveal what was going on. Within the hour, I sat down at one of the seminary's computers and typed his full unusual name into the Google search engine (led, as I now know, by the Holy Spirit); and his profile popped up on the first entry!

Upon researching this person's police file on the Internet, I discovered that he had set up and run a well-known charity in an African country, with a high profile and a high cost account, and with the money vanishing at a high rate!

He had been keeping a household in the African country, and I had already sent some money to the housekeeper, Florence, who I did speak with after these events and who also hadn't known about this man's fraudulent past or his current money-siphoning practices.

This charming old missionary had started his "religious" career at a young age. He had been the choir boy who led Prince Charles up the central church aisle in the inauguration service in Wales. And throughout his adult life, he had conned many kind and unsuspecting Christians and Christian communities.

Having been a consular clerk, I had already tried to check him out with the British Consulate, but to no avail. The sad thing is that God gave him every opportunity to get to know Him at our school, but the pretence just got worse.

The day after I had discovered this information on the Internet, I escorted Ken to see our campus pastor for a prearranged chat about supposedly giving him funds for his ministry, at which time we instead presented him with the printout from the website. He made a quick exit after trying to pretend that it was a terrible mistake and is now, I believe, in a prison back in Africa serving a long prison term for fraud.

God's lesson for me—*Beware of those who will rob you* (see Col. 2:8).

Chapter 12

Setting the Pace

And let us run with patience the race that is set before us (Hebrews 12:1b).

And so I settled into my second year at the European Theological Seminary (ETS). During the first year of classes, my fellow students had been predominantly women; there had been only four men in a group of 27 students. Then, a few of the young women moved on to other educational positions. Now, for the new school year, there were more men to balance out the previous year's uneven ratio, and…what a group!

There was a large, ex-heroin, ex-kayak champion from Serbia; a Pakistani charmer; a dark-haired, dark-eyed Romanian—a passionate, Italian-speaking fireball; among others. And they came roaring into Bible school on fire and ready to "do Jesus"!

Within the first week there had been a near revival on the staircase leading up to the different levels of the sleeping quarters. We older—and wiser—students smiled sagely and waited for the "honeymoon" to wear off! Once you are at seminary for awhile, you realize that the year always starts off with this type of energy and excitement. It's great to have the adrenaline flowing, as well as the hormones, before the reality of exams and more exams and paper writing takes its toll!

Events such as the official "Welcome to ETS" pranks arranged by the second and third-level students went ahead as they do every year. Fortunately, I had been taken out of the way by a courteous Holy Spirit the previous year; consequently, I had missed the drenching with water hoses, an inevitable part of this welcome! How I love the Holy Spirit!

It was a few weeks after the second year had started and I was sitting in class when I felt the Holy Spirit tap me on the shoulder and say, "It isn't normal to find a three-foot rainbow in your room." I had totally forgotten about the wonderful gift God had given to me the year before, and it suddenly hit me that this phenomenon was just that—a visible sign from God. It had been a miracle—a beautiful confirmation from God, giving me a "thumbs up" to remain at the seminary, against all other odds.

I sat there in my Monday morning class absolutely astounded that God had spoken to me so loudly through this colorful gift, and I hadn't even realized it. Wow! He must have been sitting on His throne, tapping His foot, waiting for me to come to my senses. Eventually, the Holy Spirit made it abundantly clear to me that this was His sign of approval. What an amazing God!

Many people from all over the world who have seen the photos of this rainbow have noticed a small triangular window on the left-hand side of the sloping ceiling. Having been married to a scientist for nearly 20 years, I happily acknowledge that the little triangular window is where the light came from to produce this beautiful sign. It is God who created light after all! If you are familiar with the Book of Genesis, you know that the rainbow (meaning "source" or "origin") is a sign of the covenant between God and man, which God gave to Noah and to all creation after the flood. As a consequence of these pictures, I was incredibly encouraged and knew that my personal Friend and Savior had spoken directly to me through this symbol of covenantal relationship. And with the photos, I made my own calling cards.

I have discussed these photos with many non-believers, and I love the look on their faces as they become aware that, if this isn't a good Photoshop print job or a fluke of nature, then maybe, just maybe, God does exist!

In the meantime, I had been asking God for the gift of heal-ing…and it started to take place. I had already been practicing the gift of healing, which hadn't been easy at first. Praying for healing without seeing results is difficult. But suddenly, healings started to happen, both small and large. I also began to notice that when I prayed with people after giving my testimony and showing them large pictures of this rainbow beautifully positioned in my room, it helped to increase people's faith. They make a good conversation opener and allow me to share the reality of Jesus and God and of miracles today. I tend to end up sitting next to non-believers, espe-cially scientific types, on planes and other forms of transportation, and interestingly they cannot explain the phenomenon.

So with this affirmation from God in hand, I began the second year of seminary with renewed hope. God had already given me an optimistic nature, and this sign was simply an additional encourage-ment in this journey for Jesus.

The apostle Paul writes in the Book of Philippians that "press to-ward the mark for the prize of the high calling of God in Christ Jesus" (see Phil. 3:14). When I had applied to the seminary, I had written this Scripture on my application form as part of the reason for wanting to attend this school. Up until this point, I had been running a very ragged race, which escalated between highs and lows.

Meanwhile, I had been given two vision pictures by two different people before leaving Scotland. Both pictures were of Jesus standing in a boat in the midst of very high choppy waves. As the waves con-tinued to toss, the presence of the Holy Spirit became ever more present and real to me. It was at this time that I started searching to know the person of the Holy Spirit better. I had read the book by

Benny Hinn—*Good Morning, Holy Spirit*; and I then found Katherine Kulhman's biography in the seminary library, recounting the miracle crusades she had led in the '60s and '70s in America. And these books fuelled my desire even more to know the Holy Spirit!

The curriculum for the second and third-level students started with a month's intensive course on the selected Bible language for that year's study. This year's curriculum included Hebrew—my first semantic language. In hindsight, I am so glad that I committed to stay at ETS, but honestly, learning this fascinating language was a slog! I have since met many people who have "done" Bible schools, and they all chuckle ruefully at the memory of studying Hebrew and Greek. I can now share in that laughter after having battled through the post-graduate courses. But once you study these languages, the Bible is never the same again—ever! To read the manuscripts in their original language and understand the formation of the inspired words of God is utterly amazing. The Scriptures come alive! I highly recommend it to anyone who wants to become more personally acquainted with God through His written Word—completely inspired.

Also during the second year, another battle within my mind took place. It was philosophy, but not philosophy as I had known it. Having studied this subject from a modern humanist perspective, I thought this subject was definitely my territory. I knew all about Plato, Aristotle, Kent, Sartre, Locke—all that true humanist stuff. But as we delved into the course material, the absolute reality of the lies of the world belief system smacked me directly in the face.

The world's philosophy is centered on man. Man is the central axle around which all else revolves. We are the ultimate creation at the top of the food chain, but…no, we do not have a creator. We are a huge universal "accident," not to mention the theory that we evolved from monkeys. But now, I had met my Creator and knew the Truth. But there were strongholds, which the devil had dug into my psychological makeup, and they were deep, very deep—that's why they are called "strongholds."

These strongholds wouldn't just crumble; they had to be dug out and destroyed as I went through this class and began to see how God had used the vehicle of philosophy to bring mankind, poor duped mankind, to a point of understanding who God is through the supernatural revelation of great thinkers like Thomas Aquinas and Augustine.

This process was incredibly painful, and the anger I experienced was indescribable. To know that mankind has been running around in circles, with ifs and buts and maybe's in the world of philosophy is disheartening. But to see the way in which God has presented the knowledge of Himself despite the lies and deceits to reach key people in each generation is fascinating and wonderful.

Meantime, in the midst of a hectic curriculum and prayer nights and general busyness of seminary life, I was called to my father as he was dying. He gave me his blessing after he made his peace with Jesus and released me to return to the seminary two days before he died. My brother and mother were with him, and God lovingly brought his favorite minister friend to his bedside to pray for him as he left this earthly life. My twin sister arrived to stay with my mother for over a month, to help her and get all the necessary paperwork in order.

I knew when I had left him that I would never see him again on earth. As I whispered, "I love you" into his ear, he in turn whispered, "I love you, too." I also knew I would see him in Heaven.

Soon, I would return to England for the funeral, which was a beautiful and stirring event. The large church was packed with over seven hundred people from all over the world coming to pay their respects. Many of these people came to the service to say how wonderful dad had been. And the only thought that I could ponder was, *What if God hadn't sent me in time to lead dad to Jesus?* He had been a wonderful person; but what is the point of being wonderful in life if death means hell for all eternity? The reality of Christ makes a mockery of our religious traditions and beliefs. Our worldly trappings and need for status are all stripped away in death. There is no second chance, and dad might have missed that, even after preaching the Gospel of Jesus Christ for years and years.

So watching and comforting all dad's congregation was a sad event for me as I listened to Christians bewailing the fact that now they had no one to bury them who knew them like my dad had. And I just wanted to wail because it's not about the funeral or who buries you, but about where you spend the rest of eternity. That's the reality of Christ.

After the funeral, I spent a few days with my family and then returned to Stansted Airport for the flight back to Germany. At this time, two significant events happened in a very short time, alerting me to the fact that my journey with Jesus was becoming more noticeable. The first was that on an already packed Ryan Air plane there were only two seats left in a row of three. The window seat had already been taken by a dark-skinned gentleman who, when we started talking, turned out to be an amazing God-connection.

I learned that he was a pastor in a church in Karlsruhe with a passion for Jesus and a hard-hitting prison ministry. We started chatting, and he told me that he had just finished attending a famous evangelist's conference in London, learning about spiritual warfare. I realized this was a God-given situation because I had wanted to go to this conference myself. Now, this pastor was passing on to me what he had learned, especially about the spirit of religion which, seeing as where I had just come from, and what I was going to be walking into, was definitely a lightbulb warning. After a wonderful time of fellowship and a powerful prayer session, the plane landed. We were pleasantly surprised when just before the landing, some prizes were handed out, and my companion won a free flight! We then parted company on arrival at Stuttgart Airport late in the evening.

Being seriously tired from all the emotional stress during the last few days, I booked into the local airport hotel instead of driving back late at night to the seminary. That night, something so radical happened that it convinced me to keep doing whatever I could do for Jesus.

After checking into the hotel room and unpacking the necessary toiletries for a one–night stay, I climbed into bed tired but relieved. As I dropped off to sleep, I was aware that there was some sort of spiritual activity going on around me, but I also knew that Jesus was watching over me and protecting me.

Sometime in the early morning hours, I woke up and immediately knew that there had been a "change" in the room. I saw a dark box, like a television set, which I could dimly make out in front of me. On one side there was the silhouette of a shadowy figure holding two children, each one sitting on his knees. What struck me instantly was that the children, also in shadow, looked like caricatures of Hansel and Gretel from the Hans Christian Anderson storybooks. As I continued to peer at this vision, the shadowy figure spoke—"These are my children. Leave them alone." I instantly knew this was satan.

The insidiousness of this meeting was vile, and I understood completely that I was being warned to back off satan's territory—mankind. The vision disappeared, and I turned over and went back to sleep. Within myself, I realized that satan has no rights over mankind when we have come to Jesus, and that the only power he has comes through using people who think that they can benefit from a relationship with hell. Chillingly, the children were totally still—a terrifying stillness that I still feel today. This visitation did not have the effect of dulling me but galvanized me to reach out even more to those who need to hear the news about Jesus and convey this news in any way in which they are best able to receive it.

When I returned to school, life intensified, as I began to help an American missionary lecturer and his group of practicum students, with a blessed yet difficult outreach in Strasbourg, France—only an hour's drive down the mountain.

The Religious Wars, which I had studied with bored indifference as a non-believer, and the history degree I had earned, now started to take on a completely different significance. My perception changed totally when I understood what was really behind the historical movements of the world and Who is in control of mankind. Yet the wars of religion have scarred the European landscape and undermined the ability of people to believe in a God, let alone a merciful and gracious God. France has become so secularized that the name, Jesus, is a laughing matter.

However, our little group of students headed into this multiracial, multi-secular, multi-religious land with the hope of setting Strasbourg on fire for Jesus.; and we were met with a brick wall of disinterest, indifference, and syncretism (in other words, all religions lead to a greater being, greater knowledge, or cosmic world—the mind). To sum it up, handing out invitations in the center of this high-profile commercial center, which houses the Council of Europe, was met with almost no response.

At one point, the youth team performed skits in the central main square. The result? Only one person attended this organized event, and he wasn't even French, but a French Canadian visitor. Yet even one person saved for Heaven is one less going to hell! So we persevered, which was just as well, as doors began to open, although through different avenues.

The consequences for me were very interesting. I made a contact with a church where I went to visit and say hello; consequently, I ended up serving with them as their internship student for my third-year practicum, which would be incredibly challenging (more about this in another chapter).

Then, it wasn't long before the Christmas season was upon us once again. The fall semester had been a long one, and everyone was excited to get dressed up and celebrate the holiday. The seminary was transformed into an elegant five-star restaurant and megaparty! We all took part in a tradition called "Wichtel," which means that each person in the seminary—students and teachers alike—pulls a name out of a hat, of whom they are to buy Christmas presents for. At that time, we were to spend up to ten euros on three presents. Two of the presents were to be hidden somewhere around the school and the third was to be opened at the Christmas party where we gathered together to sing. Some participated in drama presentations, and everyone had a fun time!

On the Wichtel day, students were busily running around, searching for their presents, and the excitement in the air was infectious. One of the lads hid his Wichtel present so high up in the ceiling of the chapel that a ladder had to be found in order to retrieve the gift. Other presents were placed in among the plants, which created a very festive look. Before the party, the chef prepared a top-rate Christmas meal fit for the best hotels in Europe! And then afterward, we all headed off to families and friends for the holidays.

This particular year, I went to my twin sister's house in Scotland, and it was good to be back and visit the church family again. The time flew by and I found myself driving back to the airport wondering what the next part of the second year would bring. Exams were scheduled in February, which meant a lot of studying and writing before that time.

As I was driving along, I suddenly realized that I had forgotten my Germany house keys and my car key, which I had left at my sister's house! In total panic, I contacted her on my German mobile phone and then turned around, heading back to meet my sister who was driving partway to meet me! What began as a relaxing trip with plenty of time to catch the flight back to Stuttgart now became fraught with anxiety. Now, I would not just have to catch one plane but two.

My sister and I met very briefly at a little Scottish village, exchanged identical expressions of stress, and then I hurtled back toward the airport, dumped the hired car outside the front door, ran through the passport control, past the duty-free lounges, and made it onto the plane with one minute to spare!

As I collapsed onto the seat, melting in a pool of fretful relief, I asked Jesus, "Am I even supposed to be on this flight?" Well, I received an answer within half an hour. The take-off had been fine, and as we soared up into the blue skies and flew over the North Sea, heading toward Schiphol Amsterdam Airport, I tried to relax. As I glanced out the little window, I was presented with an absolutely amazing sight. There below me, reflected upon banks of white clouds, was a huge outline of Jesus Christ. As I continued to stare at that figure, which had to be kilometers long and wide, I knew I had received my answer—"Yes…absolutely!" With this next fantastic sign from God, confirming that I was on the right path, I returned once again to ETS and back to life at the seminary.

In addition to studying, our brave outreach group for Strasbourg went ahead with new plans to continue to reach that city, but now we not only had to contend with the lack of enthusiasm from the French, but the poor weather as well. Our American missionary had found a youth café where we could play modern youth worship music and talk to people. In the meantime, we planned and practiced and finally headed off down the mountain in two vans and two cars.

The excitement and anticipation were great, but we met with the same lack of response as we previously had. Yet our group remained optimistic, as several young people, including a small group of Italian boys, had spoken with us and subsequently asked Jesus to become their friend. With these experiences under our belts, we now approached the final exams and the end of the second semester of the second year came hurtling to an end.

I had survived the second year with all the ups and downs of living in amongst 80 beautiful, energetic, young students whom I had come to love. We had had quite a few weddings, and now the third-year students were getting ready to go out into their practicum years.

After I had visited a church in Strasbourg and had been invited to preach by the pastor there, we agreed that that church was where I would complete my third-year practicum. This was a church which did not "do" the Holy Spirit, although their liturgy and hymns all mentioned Him alongside Father God and Jesus. I knew this experience would be a huge challenge for me, especially as I was now experiencing more people receiving healing when I prayed for them. I persevered as much as possible, knowing that the apostle Paul said "to stir up the gift of God" (see 2 Timothy 1:6)—and the only way to do this was to practice.

I had noticed that my hands would start tingling and I could feel this power trickling out of my fingers when I prayed with people. This was all very exciting and sometimes worked…and sometimes didn't. Yet there was never a question of blame in these healing prayers if nothing happened. Healing is divine; and that is Jesus' business, not mine or the person seeking the healing. We step out and Jesus steps toward us.

Then something happened that really opened up my eyes to the power of God. One of the students had taken a fall and hit his head; consequently, he heard a constant ringing noise in his head. As I passed him and his wife in the seminary one day, I felt the Holy Spirit suggesting that I pray for him. But immediately, I put the thought aside. Yet when I saw him and his wife again the next day in the library, I was again reminded that I had to pray for him. So I asked them if I could.

The husband stood in between me and his wife, and I put my hand on his forehead where he had bumped his head. The three of us were physically connected by hands when suddenly— WHUMPH! All three of us were shocked to feel the huge power surge flowing out of me! The couple looked at me with huge eyes, and I looked back at them with just as round eyes and said, "Wow— what was that?!" When the man confirmed that the ringing noise had stopped in his head, I went off. But now, I was walking around the seminary with what felt like a hole or an emptiness in my upper chest, and I didn't know what to do about it.

Eventually, I went to my mentor and she prayed for me, which helped some. Then I went to another student who prayed for me; and this time I was "filled up." It was the most amazing experience, and one that I have never experienced since. In any case, it showed me the type of power that the Holy Spirit exerts, and it reminded me of the narrative in the Bible about the woman with the issue of blood and how the power "went out" of Jesus when she had touched Him. Jesus says that we will do the same miracles and more than He ever did; and I for one know it's absolutely true (see John 14:12).

The next day the man whom I had prayed for went up during altar call at our chapel service and was laid out cold by the Holy Spirit—obviously, there was more work to be done! How I love working with the Holy Spirit—life is never dull. And on that positive note, the semester ended, and we all headed off for our summer practicum. For me, this meant pointing my car in the direction of Eastern Europe and heading to Prague, the Czech Republic.

Chapter 13

SHELTERED BY THE SPIRIT

*If I say, Surely the darkness shall cover me, even the night shall
be light around me* (Psalm 139:11).

At some point during the second year, I had noticed that my
bedroom would light up during the night; when I told our campus
pastor, he just shook his head, shrugged his shoulders, and sighed.
The faculty had almost given up trying to discern what was happening to me. When I asked God to explain what was happening, Psalm
139:11 came to mind: "*If I say, Surely the darkness shall cover me, even
the night shall be light around me.*" So I decided to accept this rather
lovely phenomenon and would nod off to sleep as usual.

In amongst seeing the light, however, I was also witnessing the
enemy. I had been told that this scene would "diminish" with time,
but this wasn't happening. The physical attacks had lessened, although the bed still shook until I kicked the mattress with my heel,
stated my authority over all the powers of darkness, and committed
myself into the hands of Jesus.

Now, as I pointed my car in the direction of Prague for my third-year practicum, I wasn't too bothered about the negative spiritual activity; I was more concerned with the practicalities of the summer arrangements. I had made plans to be in Prague so that I would be working alongside the American youth leader of the church I was a member of. I had been appointed to specifically help him organize the major youth conference for Europe that year in Maastricht, Holland. In the meantime, while waiting for his arrival in Prague, I was to teach English at the young single mothers center set up by my church as my practicum. But even before starting that, I had decided to take a couple weeks off to rest after the exams, and my mother had arranged for me to meet her in Prague for part of that time.

As I searched for a place to stay in the city, I was blessed with the opportunity of house-sitting for a missionary, whose house was located outside the city limits. I was getting used to driving a new jeep as well. The 4x4 jeep I had first driven to the seminary had become dangerous and expensive to run. I knew that the vehicle bills were getting too much for me, and so did God. I hadn't had time to find a replacement though; but in amongst all the studies, I had lifted up my wish list to Father God. This wish list included a small, two-door, dark blue 4x4 Suzuki jeep, which would be adequate for the snow conditions found on top of a mountain. My present jeep was a Range Rover Discovery and there was only one Range Rover garage nearby at Baden Baden—a good hour's drive from the seminary and located at the bottom of the mountain.

So one day, before the end of the semester, when I had to take my jeep to the shop for what looked like a seriously expensive repair job, guess what I found on the forecourt of the Range Rover garage (which sold only Range Rovers)? Yep—a 4x4, dark blue Suzuki jeep with two doors. So, who is Father God's favored daughter then? You should have seen my face. I walked around that jeep and then went to the two salesmen whom I had gotten to know quite well and said, "What is that doing here?" They informed me that someone had decided to ask for a part exchange and then left the jeep with them to sell. I asked if I could make a deal, exchanging my jeep in a purchase for the Suzuki one. They said, "Yes," and I ended up with an almost new, two-door, dark blue 4x4 Suzuki jeep. The witness to the two salesmen, Simon and Thorsten, was so cool! Later, when I told one of our young students from South Africa this story, he exclaimed, "Random!" And I replied, "Oh no, there is nothing random about God!"

So as I pointed my new jeep toward the east of Germany, I knew I was driving a divine present of a vehicle! The drive went smoothly up to the eastern border on the typically fast German motorways until I reached customs. I had never visited Eastern Europe before, and I was a little apprehensive. An American visitor at Ellel, Scotland had mentioned that the spiritual feeling of the East was another experience altogether.

As I drove into the country, I continued my usual singing, praising, and speaking in tongues—all the way to Prague. I could feel the presence of the Holy Spirit very strongly, and as I rounded the hill to see the city in front of me, tears streamed down my face. The view before me was of a light green diluting countryside marred with blocks upon blocks of grey apartment blocks.

The Orwellian imagery that I had been brought up on as a Cold War westerner came to my mind and was nearly overwhelming. I then had to tackle the ring road (similar to a beltway) around Prague to negotiate getting onto the other side of the city where Podebrady, a little town 50 kilometers east, is located. That was my immediate destination, but what a nightmare of traffic on that ring road. I have driven some challenging ring roads in my travels, but this was to be the worst yet. By the time I managed to find the little town and then the home of this missionary, with cat and plants and all, I was done in. The motorway surface from Prague to Podebrady, had totally shaken me up. It was much like the tank tracks over Salisbury Plain, which I had seen on my many journeys between my old home and my parents' home in Bournemouth, over the beautiful Cotswolds and down into the meandering countryside of Dorset.

Finally, I was able to unpack and unwind from the drive; yet there was the unsettling thought that I would have to drive all the way back around that ring road the next day when my mum arrived at the airport. (Ahhh!)

The house I was staying in was an unusual building with a two-tiered effect in the living room. The stairs to the upper part were on the inside of the wall with skylights and huge fans in the upper ceiling. As I got ready for bed and settled down to sleep with the room all lit up, suddenly there was a...wham! Wow—it was France and Germany all over again; and I had to seriously ask God why this type of experience should be happening again.

What is giving the enemy a right to do this? Why am I getting landed on all the time? What have I done wrong to deserve all this attention from the devil? I know that I love witnessing for Jesus, but many other born-again Christians do as well. I know that I have an absolute passion for Jesus, but so do many other Christians. I also know that I want to serve Him with everything I have; but don't other Christians have the same desire?

I got onto the Internet and began to establish a prayer covering. I already had one in place, but now I asked for more people to pray. This action, however, didn't stop the attacks. Then I got the idea to start searching the house, and this is when I received a very important insight. Inside this missionary's home were many games and books of which I was surprised to see. Why? There were books by Tolkien; the full set of *Lord of the Rings*; and many myths and legend genres on the bookshelves. Then, when I opened the cupboard full of games, the sense of spiritual danger caused me much additional distress.

There are actually demonic strongholds attached to these objects which, when entertained by born-again Christians, give them a foothold in those people's lives. Well-balanced, rational, reasoning, and logical Christians would disagree with me on this perspective of what is acceptable for Jesus followers to read; they argue that Jesus provides protection, and they question if any harm can actually be caused by this type of reading or gaming material. The apostle Paul writes very clearly in Second Corinthians:

For though walking about in flesh, we do not war according to flesh. For the weapons of our warfare are not fleshly, but mighty through God to the pulling down of strongholds, pulling down imaginations and every high thing that exalts itself against the knowledge of God, and bringing into captivity every thought into the obedience of Christ; and having readiness to avenge all disobedience, when your obedience is fulfilled (2 Corinthians 10:3–6).

When we entertain any form of knowledge which exalts itself above God or comes from another source rather than from God, then we entertain the devil. The devil then has every right to come into our lives. The demonic stronghold I found in this missionary's home had been permitted by the missionary himself. This was not the first time I had understood this unwitting relationship between Christians and the devil. As I opened the old wooden cupboard, the evil that hit me took my breath away! It was as if darkness actually came out of the cupboard where these games were stored and hit me in the face.

After looking at these games, I then opened the medicine cabinet in the bathroom. This time, I was not surprised but absolutely shocked to see the cabinet stuffed full of migraine headache tablets, each one containing 1000 mg. Do we know what this stuff does to our systems? I believe the Lord has revealed to me, with great concern, that when we give an entry to the devil through literature and other forms of entertainment, including computer games such as Dungeons & Dragons and the Harry Potter games, sickness then can gain a foothold in our lives. This is serious witchcraft. Books that contain evil in any way or form outside the scope of Jesus Christ are cursed deliberately by the devil and reap confusion and destruction. I have personally learned this lesson through my own need for deliverance from the literature, which I had been in bondage to prior to my conversion. Everyone needs to be aware of these dark areas of access into our lives.

After settling into this house, I began my practicum by giving English lessons to the women who ran the church's center for unmarried mothers. These women were non-believers who I managed to gently witness to, by paying attention and loving them for themselves.

I was with them for three weeks, and have acquired a lovely set of photographs of this group of women with their babies and me.

As I drove away from Prague and these delightful people, I realized that the East European countries continue to experience a deadness and a hopelessness caused by a communist regime run by the devil. The world that George Orwell wrote about condemned millions to a religion of disbelief. I do wonder how anti-God dictators will react when they die and wake up in hell.

Driving along, I was listening to the CD of the Book of Matthew where God says, "This is My beloved Son, in whom I am well pleased" (Matt. 3:17). When those words were spoken, the top of my head "moved" with the anointing of God! I had endured constant night attacks again and again, but I had managed to witness finally, and gently, to my class of "mums" before I left. I am just one follower on the road to Christ, just one of the many witnesses leading the way for others to be introduced to Jesus; therefore, it is most important that I be sensitive to the Holy Spirit. The gentle witness of a Christian led by the Holy Spirit may reap that harvest which a loud aggressive witness might destroy.

After leaving the Czech Republic, I returned to the seminary and started unpacking my suitcases at the flat I had rented in the village. I was now living in my own place for the final year, which I had really needed to finish this first leg of the race. I loved living with the students, but the age difference was a huge factor, no matter how kind and respectful they were. God knew I needed this personal space as well, so He blessed me; and I moved into a wonderful, big, airy apartment furnished from the previous students who had lived there.

When I first went to see the place and realized that they didn't want to take their furniture back home, I offered to buy it. I had asked God to give me a price to offer. When I met with these students again, they had made a list of all the items and their price…and the price God had given me was exactly the same. Don't you love it when a plan works so smoothly! So I unpacked and then headed off to Holland for the Eurofest with a mixed group of young people and students in convoy. Now that was fun!

Eurofest is a gathering together of the youth from my church organization, and presents a very colorful international representation of what Europeans look like today! Included are all nationalities, all styles, all trends—so serving for this conference was a reward in itself. I went in with my eyes wide open knowing it would be an intensive three days…and it was. There was an American group visiting who performed drama as well as who helped the Eurofest team, and all ran smoothly. Our British guests arrived and then the French and the Belgiums, the Dutch, and the Germans.

The worship bands started and the seminars also ran without a problem. And God was with us! I managed the reception areas and guarded thousands of euros for most of the time, in between practicing several languages. (My Dutch was definitely rusty!) Then I got that inkling feeling again that something was different.

As I was walking back to the reception desk, a young friend moved next to me and immediately received an electric shock that actually made her yelp! She hadn't touched me (wasn't even close), but I knew she had just received a Holy Spirit spark of power coming from me. I know now that I had and continue to have such a strong desire and determination to be so at one with God and that God is determined to be with me. I want God to live in me, with me, around me, to flow through me—and it is this desire to be so yielded to our living God that motivates my whole life.

To be with our Creator God is almost indescribable. Yet I will attempt to explain to give you an idea of how beautiful our God is! After Eurofest, I went to visit some friends in Belgium and was asked to minister to a friend of the family—a young lady who came from Pakistan and had received Jesus but was having difficulties with the spiritual side. I went to visit her and pray with her; and through the leading of the Holy Spirit, we started to unravel her very disturbed past and dark areas of her life.

I met with this woman several times and discovered another aspect of the deliverance ministry for which God also began to train me. After the last session with her, I later woke up from the most fantastic dream or vision. I saw myself on the edge of a deep sea pool—the type of pool you see at seaside resorts where you can swim out to sea or stay close to the pool edge. A voice said, "You can get in." So I got in, and as I did so, three dolphins swam up to me and took me out into the deep waters.

What did this mean? When you let go and swim with the Holy Spirit, then nothing can affect you. No waters are too deep to dive into when you are going with the Spirit of God. It was then that I finally realized that I am having a relationship with the Spirit of God who has created everything, and He wants to look after me and every single person who will listen to the message of salvation in Jesus. This is the reality of Christ.

Chapter 14

PATCHING THOSE
CRACKED POTS!

Looking to Jesus the Author and Finisher of our faith (Hebrews 12:2a).

I returned to my new flat in the village with some holiday time left to catch my breath before the next semester started. Now that I was living in my own place, some things were different. For example, I chose to do my own cooking, so I was no longer joining everyone for the communal meals. And it was at this point that the Holy Spirit stepped in with the answer to my ongoing struggle with social drinking. I had been battling with this issue until finally, God gave me the key, and I unlocked the door. Just as with smoking, I was able to give this addiction totally over to Jesus.

I had been out shopping, and as I carried my purchased items into the kitchen, I was saying to the Holy Spirit, "Now for a nice glass of wine and relaxation." A reply came back instantly, "But you won't relax; you will go into a struggle because you are a born-again Christian and not the person you used to be." I realized immediately that the Holy Spirit was right.

Before my conversion it didn't matter how much I drank. I belonged to the devil; therefore, drinking too much or not drinking at all meant nothing, because in either case, a non-believer remains on the road to hell. But as for Christians who are on fire for Jesus, the devil seriously wants to make sure we are not only tempted, but baited, and then caught and shamed by secret (or not so secret) habits. These were exactly my circumstances.

The Holy Spirit gave me two keys. First, He reminded me that drinking alcohol is not a form of relaxation for a born-again Christian, whose pre-Jesus life style revolved around social drinking. Second, I am not the person I used to be. After two years of struggling, by my own choice, in the Bible seminary, God finally gave me the key when I was living outside the rules of the Bible school and I could do what I wanted.

And what I wanted to do was live at peace—a peace that only Jesus can give. Once I found that peace, my life changed completely.

In the meantime, two weeks prior to the beginning of the semester, the second and third-level students once again attended an intensive Bible language course. This time we were learning Greek, and it was just as painful an experience as Hebrew had been the year before. But then again, lists and lists of words to learn and grammar to comprehend made for quite a bonding experience with 40 young people!

Then it was the first day of the official semester and we all were back in the large and spacious seminary chapel with its walls of windows opening upon the view of the mountaintop and surrounding woods.

God gave us an inkling of His thoughts for that new semester during the first student devotion for the year. A third-year student presented a thought about the people of God being used as His vessels, and addressed our personal relationship with our loving Father God. She used pots and vases to demonstrate her message.

Then it was my turn. One of the young students, Vicky, who is like a daughter to me, always translated my messages into German. She and I were dressed nicely and stood side by side.

I started my message by holding up a crazy orange, yellow, red, and white vase and asking everyone, "How is your cracked pot today?" The young audience laughed appreciatively; we all were reminded in that chapel service how God patches His cracked pots! My message continued and I reminded everyone of how we can trust God in all things. In Philippians, the apostle Paul speaks to the congregation of Philippi and tells them, very reassuringly:

> *"Do not be anxious about anything, but in everything by prayer and supplication, with thanksgiving, let your requests be made known to God. And the peace of God which passes all understanding shall keep your hearts and minds through Christ Jesus"*(Philippians 4:6-7).

Seven, simple, sequential steps were used by this wise man of God. The first is not to be anxious; the second is to do everything by prayer; the third by supplication; the fourth with thanksgiving; the fifth is to make all needs known to God; which then results in the sixth step—God's peace and understanding; and the ultimate result is the seventh step—our hearts and minds are kept in this mode by Jesus. It is Jesus who helps us to accomplish these seven steps.

Simple. That is what our God is about—simplicity. I kept their attention by walking down the chapel steps in time with the seven steps I was teaching on, and back up them again, making the perfect count of seven. The audience helped me to count off the steps and repeated them out loud   bless them! I knew that a few fellow students were also holding their breath in case I tripped! To complete the devotion, I felt the Holy Spirit encouraging me to pray a general healing prayer.

A short time later in the day, I started to hear of healings that had happened as the students sat in their seats during the concluding prayer, and I knew then that as I preached His Word, God was entrusting me with more of His healing power, just as He had given to Katherine Kuhlman.

God was also entrusting me with the mentoring of His students; more and more the young students would come to me for prayer and encouragement. Psalm 113:9—"He causes the barren to dwell in the house as a joyful mother of sons. Praise Jehovah!" was starting to become a reality. This fact was brought home by Sandra. God had used her to speak to me on several occasions, and at one point she looked at me and said, "You know, you are more like our mum." I nearly cried and had to go off into a corner so as not to start blubbering in the middle of the seminary. In addition, some of the younger men would also come for prayer. I really felt like they were my own sons. These relationships provided a personal healing for me as well. It was also Sandra who would be the one to give me the first hint of what God was preparing me for next.

One afternoon, the representatives of a very highly respected military chaplaincy division managed by the Church of God came to see us at the seminary from the American military base in northern Germany. They shared a good presentation, which was highly charged with the God-given directive to serve in whatever field we are placed in.

Later, as I was walking out of the chapel where the presentation had taken place, Sandra stopped me and said, "You'd make a good chaplain." I looked at her with raised eyebrows and a surprised look. My father had been a chaplain, but I had never thought about personally being one. Yet that suggestion would be one that would soon return to mind.

Meanwhile, as an internship student, I was now travelling down and back up the mountain every Sunday to meet with the International Church of Strasbourg. The journey to the bottom of the mountain is about two miles of continuous hairpin bends, and then there is a mixture of country and motorway roads before arriving to this city, which is the seat of the Council of Europe.

The group of people in this church came from many different denominational backgrounds. I had first understood that this church was a Baptist-led congregation, but my knowledge of American churches soon proved that I needed to do more research. This church was started up by Southern Baptists but then split off and became an ecumenical church belonging to a group called AICEMEA, an association of Christian congregations whose members choose to worship in diverse styles, traditions, denominational affiliations, and membership. Many of these churches were started by Christians from North America, and the reverend who leads this church today is from the American Baptist Churches, USA.

The membership of these churches worldwide is mainly English-speaking expatriates who are living and working abroad. They are made up of professionals, diplomats, and a core group of resident foreigners. So I found myself, ironically, in a church very much like the one that my father had ministered to in Amsterdam. This situation was very challenging indeed, and I had to dig in deep, asking God for His strength. I was the only Pentecostal in that fellowship, which had been damaged by a schism two years before when the fundamentalist group within had departed in anger. When I found out about this unfortunate incident, I realized that I had to tread carefully. Building bridges is all about placing the bricks precisely and cautiously, and I now realized that God was calling on me to learn how to minister in amongst different denominations without causing doctrinal or theological offence while also standing firm in my own beliefs.

Before I joined the Strasbourg church, I had received three vision pictures from God to help me with this ministry. These visions were sequential. The first showed a man sitting at a table signing an official-looking document; the second picture was of a narrow cylinder which then was sliced in half; and the third was a picture of a man putting this document into a deep inside pocket of an overcoat. I phoned the campus pastor and his wife about these visions, and they invited me to come and pray and talk with them immediately.

After doing so, the pastor explained the simple message from God. It was God who was signing the agreement between myself and this non-Pentecostal church; therefore, it was His responsibility. The second picture was of the covenant or the agreement form, placed in a special tube container being cut in two. This was referring to the different kinds of treaties in the Old Testament that were made between the countries in power during that era. And the third picture was of God pocketing the agreement form, placing it deeply and protectively so that no one could tamper with it. These pictures were a true blessing that I received the day before I started working with the church.

This group of people was such a challenge for me because they represented a cross-section of the people whom I was involved with prior to my conversion—scientists, space scientists, and philosophical evolutionists who believed that mankind evolved from apes, that God is a disinterested creator God, or He may actually be interested but too far away to help mankind in their day-to-day existence. The need for logical reasoning in faith is understandable by world thinking systems; but applying empirical methodology to faith belief is something (I have discovered myself) almost impossible. One can reason as much as one wants, but without faith, you will not be able to believe that Jesus, whom you can't see, is standing in the same room as you. My father also believed that God was a faraway God who had done His bit by sending Jesus to die for us. In the meantime, He was sitting on His throne, leaving us to get on with it.

It's also very difficult to preach to people who don't believe in the original separation of mankind from God—what is known in the Bible as "The Fall." This was a concept I had found difficult to accept as well—I didn't like it. To know that some people thousands of years ago were responsible for my state of being guilty—and I didn't even know I was guilty—was horrendous. It's appalling to realize that we are personally guilty, because as rational-reasoning human beings we automatically blame other people. It's never our fault; it's always someone else's. But as the truth of this reality entered into my soul, I also realized God's overwhelming grace and kindness toward us, His lowly creation. Pride and rebellion are the marks of satan; he was the first to rebel and seek God's position. But now, he has been utterly defeated by the shameful and agonizing death that Jesus endured on the cross.

At the International Church of Strasbourg, I was kindly allowed to preach frequently, and I enjoyed getting to know this fellowship and interact with them. One of the ladies allowed me to pray and lay hands on her twice, and subsequently, she received healing twice. We came to the understanding that going to the doctor or the physiotherapist was still a good idea, and I agreed gently because I knew that faith healing sometimes causes uncertainty and fear, because if it doesn't work, many people think it is their fault. This is a sad reflection, because God heals in different ways—by miracles, which can be instantaneous, or in other ways that might take a little longer. God uses varied ways and methods of His gifts and talents to help us be healthy. After all, He made the medicinal plants and gave us the intelligence to study them!

But what I finally realized was just how gentle God was being with these people. Every sermon I felt led to preach had the same message—God wants to know you on a one-to-one basis. I know that God is a good and gentle person and that I am only one of the people to whom God extends reconciliation.

I cannot express enough my deep gratitude to this group for their friendship and trust in allowing me to minister to them and come alongside them. I truly hope that my time with them helped to mend the painful memories of the schism that occurred between them and the fundamentalist group who left. I believe God brought me to them to show that Pentecostals don't want schisms; God wants His people to build bridges.

The third year went past so quickly between the Strasbourg practicum, the early morning lessons, and the studying and writing that was starting to really wear me down before Christmas break. I had already realized that I was trying to accomplish too many goals, and the load was becoming too heavy. I ended up going back to Scotland a week early for Christmas just to recuperate. This idea of recovery was a nice one, and I've also realized that a change can be as good as a rest. For when I walked into my twin sister's house, I was met by her little grandson, and life went from being extremely busy to being extremely grandson busy! Oh boy! This lively little boy had come to live with my sister and her husband full-time, and they became his legal guardians. He was a ball of energy! So this Christmastime was fun. My mother joined us, which was particularly necessary because this was the first Christmas without dad, and we needed each other's support.

During this time, I had arranged to return to Scotland to complete my practicum year, and I was lined up for some local preaching. It was good to be back home with my first church family; I really appreciated being with them again. This arrangement to return to Scotland had been a "Kirstie plan"; I didn't know what God wanted me to do, so I was knocking at different doors to see which one looked like the "God plan."

One of the reasons I thought the return might possibly be the wrong plan was because I knew that Jesus Himself hadn't been accepted by His own people in His own country. Moreover, God was encouraging me more and more in faith healings. A prayer I had led at the Strasbourg church for a young man in Canada with cancer came back answered within that week—no sign of cancer when he went for his next hospital check-up. In addition, other healings inside and outside of the Bible seminary were now taking place on a regular basis. One young lady had been in a car accident years ago; we prayed and she was completely healed from all pain. At first the healing had been partial; subsequently, we continued to press in.

I had been reading about divine healing, and learned that if we continue to pursue God's healing when it is "in the house," then we will succeed. So we continued praying and rebuking that pain, telling it to go; consequently, the healing power increased, and she was totally healed.

There was another young lady in a hospital, who was in extreme pain and waiting for a back operation to repair an upper disc problem in her spine. I prayed for her, binding the pain, chucking it out of her body, and believing that the pain would depart. At the moment I prayed for her in belief, the pain left. The one important fact to mention is that I prayed this prayer over one hundred kilometers away from the hospital. Within minutes, she then texted her friend who prayed with me to tell us the pain had gone. And other healings, little and not so little, continued.

At this point, I said to Jesus, "Are You sure You want me here in Scotland?" These people know me, and perhaps like the people who knew You, they'll never believe" (see Mark 6:5). Later that week, at the church service on Sunday, a kind, lovely woman asked if we could pray for her boyfriend. As we did, she suddenly started shaking, and I started thinking, *Help, Holy Spirit. What are You doing?!* The next moment, she was up dancing and running around, touching her toes and accomplishing all sorts of feats! She had been in physical pain for years, and in that one moment of prayer, while we were praying for help for another person, Jesus completely healed her. This is *our* God!

A few days later at my sister's house, we were having dinner with a visiting friend. He had hurt his shoulder, and as he was explaining his pain to me, I felt a light fluttering over my finger knuckles on my right hand. This interesting feeling had been a new signal from the Holy Spirit that I had only just started to pick up, which meant that "healing was in the house"—that is how I now describe any healing moment, referring also to the power available to Jesus, as is recorded in Luke 5:17b: "And the power of the Lord was there, for the curing of them" (KJV).

I immediately responded to this invitation by the Holy Spirit and asked our friend if he wanted to pray for healing. He did, and I laid my hand on his shoulder. Afterwards, he said that his entire shoulder went icy cold, and then the pain simply left. My twin sister had been watching and now said, "Okay, my turn next—my lower back." Before we started to pray, she mentioned that someone had once laid their hands on her for healing, before she was a Christian, but it was not from Jesus. It hadn't worked, and her back continued to torment her. Now, she felt led to ask for forgiveness for having gone to the wrong source for healing. When we prayed, she also felt an icy coldness in her lower back, and then the pain disappeared.

Next, my brother-in-law, who had pulled his chest muscles, stepped up; and again we prayed. Nothing appeared to happen, but the next morning he reported that he had no pain whatsoever. God doesn't always work right away. Three of my close family and friends in a row! What do you think God was telling me?

One other healing was simply amazing. A friend of ours, who was going to Cambodia as a missionary with her husband and children, had had back surgery; unfortunately, the surgeon had left a sliver of bone in her back. This was causing her so much pain and distress that she had consequently lost all feeling in her left leg. I went to visit her with my twin sister and just sat with my hand on her asking Jesus to heal her. When we left, she was running up and down the street and jumping up and down. These are only a few of the wonderful healings that Jesus has permitted me to be a part of.

By the time I returned to the Bible seminary, I was in need of more rest! Holy Spirit is awesome; but He doesn't need to sleep, and I do! God started working on me in this area of being too busy in a nonstop world. He has shown me that there is a way to be busy without burning out. The Hebrew word for "rest" is *shabbat*, which God reminds me of frequently. I have discovered that the only way to rest is by being systematically organized and focused on the list of "must dos" versus the list of "can wait." By prioritizing carefully, all things can be accomplished and achieved through Christ Jesus.

Routine life at the seminary was once again intensive with exams, yet life went quiet-ish again until the word "chaplaincy" returned. This word had resurfaced in my mind from time to time, and I would then go off and research information regarding how to do chaplaincy with the Church of God in Europe. Subsequently, I'd find nothing and then return to my studies. At times, I would casually and briefly mention this outcome to my female mentor at the seminary who is an American chaplain, but we were so busy that we never met up to discuss the situation more thoroughly. Then God brought the reason to the surface.

Every winter, just after the Christmas break, we would receive our usual visit from the Youth Christian Education leader from our American founding church. This time, he brought a team with him from the U.S. to conduct workshops regarding how to maximize a children's ministry. I had been given the task of helping this team the previous year after their visit to the seminary when they would hold another conference in another country.

The first time I helped, we went up to the Netherlands to the Dutch churches and had a wonderful time there. On their next visit to the seminary, during my third year, I was again invited to be the tour aide, this time visiting our Parisian churches. This turned out to be another wonderful and beneficial visit, and it was after this visit that the next steps of my journey with Jesus were orchestrated.

On the day that we drove the American team back to Stuttgart Airport and said fond and grateful farewells, I would never have guessed that I would be seeing our team leader again—and sooner than I had expected.

The next day was a holiday, and I decided to give the whole day to my Father God to find out what His plan for me might be. You see, I had now come to the absolute understanding that God had a particular and special plan for me…and I wanted to be in that plan. He has a special plan for each one of us if we will only get to know Him. And when we do, then we can enter into and live in that promised land.

As soon as that day started, I knew I had to look at the seminary website, and specifically for the seminary in America. And guess what? I found that there were courses for a Master of Divinity at the American seminary leading to…Chaplaincy. Now for some people, this might have been an obvious information site to go to as a member of this huge church founded in America. But I had been so busy looking in Europe that I hadn't thought to look at what our American seminary was offering. Also, to be perfectly honest, I never even thought about going to America—I have always been a dedicated European.

So after much consultation with my mentor and with the other faculty staff, I applied; and within a few months, I received my acceptance to start at the American seminary in August 2008. Chaplaincy would be God's goal plan for the next step of my journey.

This change from the "Kirstie plan" to the "God plan" certainly changed the last part of my semester at the European Theological Seminary. While papers and exams were again looming, the third-level students also had to plan our leaving party from the seminary. Now papers and exams were again looming but the third level students also had to plan our leaving party at the Seminary. Each year the third year does this which finalizes those three years of studying together on a mountain top. This was a time of hope and expectation combined with a tinge of sadness and uncertainty; we were about to be released out into the big world which, as our president had informed us, would not be so nice to us as the seminary had been.

My fellow students had taken the news of my next step in different ways. Some were obviously astounded at the idea of my leaving Europe; others were delighted; and others said it was what they had expected! All I knew was that it "felt right," just as the decision to go to ETS had felt right three years previously. The rightness of it all was then capped by my visa application visit to Frankfurt. This large city lies north of Stuttgart and a couple hours drive from the seminary, so I decided I would book into a hotel overnight in order to be fresh and on time for the nine o'clock appointment at the American Embassy.

As I was unpacking in my room at the hotel, I thought I would first rest a bit and then go down to the lobby where there was Internet and e-mail access. This sounded like a good plan, but then the Holy Spirit gave me the distinct impression that I should go to the lobby now, and not later. Because I always want to be in the right place at the right time, which is why I listen carefully for what the Holy Spirit wants to do, I went. What happened next honestly amazed me.

I had logged online, and within a short time there was a woman standing next to me. I started chatting with her and found out that she was Scottish and had come to work in Frankfurt in a job she had

had a year previously. She also needed access to the Internet, so I proceeded to finish. While I was doing so, we continued to share more information, and I discovered she needed to go into town, but had no car. I felt the leading of the Holy Spirit, so I offered to take her in mine with the understanding that she would do the guiding because I didn't have a map of the city. Then she told me her name and I stopped short, because her name was one that I had been receiving from the Holy Spirit to pray for during the last few months. She didn't have a German name, so I had wondered who this person would be and what was happening in her life. I was about to find out.

I don't believe in coincidences in the Kingdom of God, so I knew something special was about to take place. We continued to talk more in the car on the way into town and while walking around the shops looking for food. It was a holiday and the only place to buy food was in the railway station supermarket. After she completed her shopping, she wanted to continue to walk, so I offered to take her purchased items back to the hotel and meet up with her later.

When she returned to the hotel, she came to get her food, and we sat down for a cold drink and a chat. She had already asked me about myself earlier, and I had told her without reservation about my life and what had happened to me since Jesus came and spoke to me. We had previously spoken about my experiences, but this time it was as if a dam had burst.

This young woman had been going through hell, the same type of torment I had endured before Jesus spoke to me. And she was very, very close to the edge of a nervous mental breakdown. She wanted to know about Jesus as she partially believed that He existed, but just like I thought, she was confused and misguided about who He really is. We talked a while longer and then went our separate ways. As I walked away, I knew that Jesus had put me in her pathway to let her know who He is. But before we left, I prayed for her and subsequently was given another female name—a name that I had thought of and prayed for previously. This lady would turn out to be standing behind me in the queue the next day at the embassy.

She asked the same questions about Jesus, and I knew once again that I had been used to touch another atheist on the path of life for Jesus. This is what is so amazing about God—He reaches out and wants to touch every single person on this planet so as to save them from hell. Jesus says that His Father God does not want to lose any of us to eternal damnation. Rather, He wants to bring all of us safely to Him.

My visa interview proceeded so quickly that I was out of the embassy within a few hours and driving back to the seminary. I was required to leave my passport at the embassy, which made me feel very strange. I never like being without my identity document, but it was returned quickly. And when I opened the envelope, I was in for a real shock. Gabi, my friend and mentor, was standing behind me when I said, "Look, Gabi, I got the visa." And upon looking at it, she started laughing! When I inquired why, she told me to look at the duration for the visa. It wasn't for three years as I had expected, but for five! *But why for five years?* I wondered. Gabi nodded seriously and said, "Ask God." Asking God is a wise action to take as a believer—and as a non-believer—because you never know, He might well answer you.

Chapter 15

BEING AT PEACE

Jehovah is my strength, and my fortress, and my deliverer; my God, my rock; I will trust in Him; He is my shield, and the horn of my salvation, my high tower (Psalm 18:2).

Psalm 18:2 describes my position in Jesus now—He's my strength; my fortress; my deliverer; my God; my rock; my trust; my shield; my salvation; and my high tower! Since first hearing the voice of God in 2004, I have finally come to understand that I can trust Him, that I can believe Him, that I can cast all my fears and worries onto Him.

Part of getting to know Jesus was visiting Israel during the summer of 2008 to see the places where He grew up and lived. It was a strange holiday for me actually. Prior to this trip, I had completed my practicum in Prague, moved into the new flat in the village, then travelled to Maastricht, Holland for the Eurofest Conference, and back to the village. Now, I was taking a journey to Israel with a group of Germans and Romanians. And no, I didn't speak much German and absolutely no Romanian at all! So why did I go? I felt I needed to—the Holy Spirit had led me to "go" on this trip organized by the seminary's president and his wife, Paul and Gabbi.

In hindsight, it was a necessary trip to have taken, because now I better understand where Jesus, the person, came from. The Jordan Valley is beautiful, and the desert mountains create an overwhelming feeling of an aching loss—a bleakness beautiful in its own right. We toured with two coaches, drivers, and guides who were not Christians, but Jews. It was ironic to have Jewish tour guides tell us about Jesus, especially because we had so many pastors and Bible school students on board! There were some points of disagreement between the guides and us from time to time, and I know that the presence of 70-plus Christians full of the Holy Spirit started to have an effect on them!

One of the excursions was to Mount Carmel where Elijah challenged the priests of Baal, who God soundly thrashed (see 1 Kings chapter 18). We had started out early, and at this stop, the two coach groups split up. The German group was ahead of us; and I was part of the second group, which included the Romanians, two other Bible school students, and Gabbi. When we arrived at Mount Carmel, the first group was already leaving, and we found the view stunning.

After some time there and before we made our way back down toward the coach, the Romanian pastor wanted to conduct a short service in the chapel on the top of the Mount. So we all went into this small building and started praising Jesus and singing, "Open the eyes of our heart, Lord." Our Jewish tour guide, Isaac, attempted to hurry us along (which he had continually tried to do the entire trip). But then, the presence of the Lord manifested in that building, and we just stood there and praised Him. When we left, Isaac had tears in his eyes. I'm sure he experienced something especially different that day.

Later, we floated on the Dead Sea, climbed the mountain of Masada, and held another service on top of that mountain in the fort amongst the ruins where 960 Jewish Zealots held out with their families for three years against the Roman army, before committing suicide en masse, rather than being taken alive by the enemy.

The experience of being a coach tourist rather than a coach director, was another learning curve for me. And God used this experience to show me in His gradual healing process, how to be a part of the group rather than the leader. As a tour director of many tours when I was in my 20s, I was accustomed to being the leader on coach tours, but now I was part of the group being led. This was a novel experience, and one which I am still not sure how I feel about. But I did take the opportunity to tell the guides and the driver of our coach that I had been "one of them," and used that conversational piece as a way to eventually talk to them about Jesus.

Also during this trip, I found Christine Darg's book, *The Jesus Visions*, in a Galilean bookshop. I had heard about this ministry in the Middle Eastern countries, so I bought a copy and settled down to read about Jesus appearing to the Muslims and Jews in these areas. The effect of this book on me while being there opened up new insights and revelation. I was able to witness for Jesus to a number of Jews whom the Holy Spirit touched and brought to me in special ways, including an Israeli woman in the hotel where I was staying.

God had given me the sign of His covenant, the rainbow, especially in times of the worst attacks. And when I again saw a rainbow in this hotel lobby, I was delighted! It appeared very early in the morning and actually ran straight across the whole length of the 24-foot glass panelling—which is just not feasible to any logical-reasoning human being! I thought I was the only one who had seen the rainbow *inside* the hotel lobby; therefore, I thought it was just for me. But no, Jesus was reaching out to this young woman as well.

When I mentioned this rainbow, she sheepishly admitted that she had seen it, too. I looked at her in a knowing way and said, "You know that God is chasing you." It wasn't a question; she already knew. And I had the privilege of being the person to tell her the first part of the Jesus story.

After the main group had left Israel, I stayed on alone and had been fasting and praying for three days in the Tel Aviv hotel. I knew I would be preaching on my return to Europe, and I wanted to provide the right message for an international church. On the second night of fasting, I received a vision in the early hours of the morning—I saw myself handing something to a young woman, and I could see it was a piece of A4 paper.

In reality, at the end of my stay in Israel, I actually handed my last A4 photograph of the rainbow, which God had placed in my Bible seminary bedroom, to this same young woman. Wonderful! I didn't realize until later that this is what I had seen in my vision.

I never go anywhere without pictures of this rainbow. They provide a wonderful testimony and witness of God's covenant and faithfulness, which helps to increase the faith of both those people who believe and who don't believe. And then we are able to pray for many issues, including divine healing—both theirs and mine, which brings much fruit!.

God tells us directly through His Word that we will experience many trials and tribulations for His name's sake, that we all will experience a proving time, which is different for each one of us, depending upon what God has in mind for us. And although I don't know why, some of us will experience a more difficult time than others.

But in the second year at seminary, I knew that God had already lined me up for something unique when a beloved young graduate student, who was leading his own very dynamic church in northern Germany, stopped next to me and said, "God is lifting you up into a ministry of the prophetic and of intercession." I said, "Okay." Then he paused, looked at me with his startling, piercing blue-gray eyes and continued, "Oh yes, you'll also be teaching spiritual warfare," to which I replied, "Of course!" He then concluded with the words, "Be bold." I needed to be bold in witnessing for Jesus, for eternity has no end.

Later that day I had a very strong prayer session with this young man, and we both shared our hell experiences, which God had allowed us to go through. This young pastor had been asked and hesitantly agreed to conduct a funeral service for a person who hadn't known Jesus. He didn't know what he should say at the actual service, but as he walked to the graveside, God told him where these people were headed and opened this pastor's ears so that he could hear the screams of the souls in hell. As he told me this story, his eyes revealed his torment. I then told him about what had happened to me on my journey into hell.

Later, during my third year at the seminary, this young man came back to visit. Although he had seen hundreds if not thousands of people in his ministry, he still had a specific prophecy to share with me. He looked me directly in the eyes and repeated the message God had given to me through him the previous year—exactly the same words, word for word. Included were the Scriptures that I have been given time and time again—Psalm 17:8 stating that God literally shelters us under His wing, and Psalm 91:1 assuring me that I can rest under the shadow of the Almighty King. He is not some far-distant God sitting on a throne ignoring His subjects. Instead He is an almighty God who is also a very concerned and loving Father to us all.

One of the devotions I gave at the seminary one time was about keeping our eyes fixed on Jesus all the time because the path that leads to eternal life with Jesus is very narrow. Just because I am on that path today doesn't mean I won't fall down. And if my eyes are not continually fixed on Him, then satan will do everything to drag me back down to his level. Does this mean we can lose our salvation? I do not know; I do not have that answer. I do know that my God is an awesome God who is kind, loving, and righteous. He does not want to lose any of us. But can we cause ourselves to be lost? Again, I don't have an answer. The apostle Paul does warn us, very pointedly, however, to "work out our salvation with fear and trembling" (Phil. 2:12b KJV). I continue to remember that Jesus bought me with the price of His life. I know what hell feels like; and although I was there for only a short visit, I don't want to go there ever again.

The narrative that Jesus gave about the ten virgins and the oil in their lamps is very direct and clear about how I, as a born-again Christian, must maintain my relationship with Jesus. That story in

Matthew chapter 25 is directed to Christians who already have the Holy Spirit. The oil represents the level of their relationship with Jesus. Through this example, I understand that Jesus is giving me a warning. I must keep my oil supply filled and overflowing through a constant relationship with my God, with His Holy Spirit, in the presence of His Son, Jesus every day. When you bathe in the Son, you receive the glory!

So now I had made my way through the third year and experienced the "delights" of learning Greek. (Actually, I thought Hebrew might have been easier, although my course grades don't agree!) And I started to come to other realizations, of which the most interesting was that coming to Jesus from the world of an atheist actually allowed me to believe that God really can do anything and everything. The problem had been trusting Him. What I went through prior to my conversion destroyed not only my brain cells through the abuse of world living, but also destroyed all my trust in anyone or anything. It has been only since 2004 that I have realized that I can *trust God.*

Doesn't it sound pitiful not to trust the Creator of the universe? But even more amazing is that God has trusted me! He put me into an environment of boisterous love and surrounded me with so much activity that I never had time for self-pity. Indeed, the challenge of studying while not getting much sleep was demanding; but again, He led me to know that I couldn't do it without Him. So, actually, it was His problem! This attitude was quite an interesting perspective for someone who was used to being in control and who didn't want to feel controlled by other people, let alone by a proclaimed living God.

Our postmodernism has gone mad as our perspective of living is all about "me." I came from that self-absorbed attitude where I, even when helping others, had to be gratified, to make me feel better. The book, *Selfish Gene*, written by Richard Dawkins, best summarizes the world I had lived in when it describes the idea that a chicken serves only as the eggs' way of being reproduced; this is the basic tenet of survival and life.

I had a delightful conversation with one of the students about that serious philosophical question, "Which came first—the chicken or the egg?" My idea was that the hen was created with the eggs already inside her. But when I shared this idea with Vicky, she looked at me with that beautiful, surprised look that only a young, unsullied, truly innocent, in-love-with-God person can, and replied, "God made both the hen and the cock," taking the sting out of this sad philosophical debate. Another stronghold just got dashed to smithereens.

Chapter 16

RESTING IN THAT PEACE

Peace I leave with you, My peace I give to you. Not as the world gives do I give to you. Let not your heart be troubled, neither let it be afraid (John 14:27).

You might be relieved to finally read that these days, I don't get jumped upon quite as much! I know I feel better! Yet when I do something unwittingly wrong, it can open a door to the enemy, but the Holy Spirit helps me to close it as quickly as possible. This doesn't mean that the Holy Spirit always shows me what the problem is immediately. We humans do learn best sometimes by experience. Moreover, sometimes I haven't been in the right listening mode or used the correct transmitter. However, my fine-tuning is getting better all the time, and there is something I do know for absolutely sure—I'm in love with Jesus.

This swearing, cursing, ex-atheist daughter of two generations of preachers is head over heels in love with this Man from Galilee. There is an old song referring to the Man of Galilee, which was quoted to me when I was in Tiberius; and this song has stuck in my memory ever since.

One day, in the earlier days of my walk, when the attacks were so bad that nothing made sense, and people were blaming me for what was happening, I asked Jesus if I could just go home. Then that night I received a dream vision. I saw myself standing next to a huge round door, and as I looked through it, the light was so bright that it was literally blinding. In that instant, the door swung shut and I was left in utter darkness.

I shared this vision at one of our youth conferences at ETS, called "Wake Up," during the New Year's season. Hundreds of young people had come to the Bible seminary to pray in the New Year together. This gathering was—and continues to grow bigger and bigger, and is—a great and powerful meeting with this vision and Jesus gave me an insight into this darkness, which He wants me to always share.

Although our world is wrapped in darkness, there is a great light gathering in different areas of the world. This light is made up of many lights, representing the people of God. Each one of us is filled with the light of Jesus; and when we come together, that light burns stronger. This is the end-time picture of our earth wrapped in the light of Jesus Christ.

Every morning, when we pick up our crosses anew, we pick up the light of Jesus. In turn, if we lay them down, we dim the light of His image in the world. Hence, it is so important to renew our minds, which means to reeducate our minds each new day. Each day is, literally, a new day for the Lord during which more and more people are being saved for the Kingdom of God.

I now know for sure that my journey from atheism to the cross of Jesus Christ is being secured every day by the sacrifice of Jesus. I have laid down the science fiction, fantasy, humanism, Darwinism, and every other world "ism" and have taken up the cross of Jesus. I have arrived fully in the reality of Christ. The religion of atheism has lost; the reality of Christ has won.

It was the providence of God and no accident when I first drove up to my sister's home in Scotland, after leaving my old life. My father, who was a man of God but affected by a spirit of religion, called my twin sister while I was driving up to her, and told her she was not to speak to me about Jesus in my vulnerable state of mind. Please understand that my father, my loving and kind dad, told his daughter, my sister, not to speak to me about Jesus or His gift of salvation. My father knew I didn't believe in Jesus; he knew I was an atheist. In the meantime, I had the choice between going to my parents' house and my sister's house on the day I left my ex-husband. My parents' home was only a few hours away, whereas my sister's home was hundreds of miles away. Why is it that I turned my jeep in the direction of her born-again life?

I now realize that there was a continual godly interception. Why was it, years ago, when I was moving out of my parents' house in Amsterdam to go and live with my husband-to-be, that I looked at myself in the mirror in my bedroom and saw something strange in my eyes? At that instant, I felt compelled to look closer, but then the thought came to get on with moving out, so I immediately forgot all about it. And why was it, years later, at my home in Feckenham, while I was staring at myself in despair in the mirror, looking into my eyes again, as I had done in Amsterdam, that Jesus spoke to me in that split second?

Even though I know I wouldn't have wanted to see what was really there, still God's timing is perfect. When I told a Holy Spirit-filled sister about this experience, she received the word, "self-destruction." I was on the road to hell when Jesus intervened.

If any person should read this account of my progress as a non-believer from the hell of atheism to the Kingdom of God, then may I offer you an insight? In the genre of science fiction and fantasy, where do you think all those stories come from about lost worlds, intergalactic space travel, wormholes, weird puppet-like creatures, time travel discs, agony-spiked trees with human beings writhing on them eternally, inner space and outer space, fantasy-floating islands and trees, robotics, robots, the end of the world, the foundation at the end of the universe, and on and on? Do you really believe that mankind could ever have had the creative imagination to be able to come up with such a dark side of science fiction fantasy?

To look up at the stars and not see God is the saddest experience a human being can ever live through—and that was me. To look up at the stars and not realize that the God who made them also made us with the love and care and attention that He paid to them is demonic and evil. The cause of universal destruction is not God's choice but man's choice to separate from God as a result of a desperate state called sin. Just as faith has substance, so does sin have a substance. The weight of sin is destroying all of us, including you.

In the first summer of my new life with Jesus, I saw a vision of something I couldn't understand at the time. It looked like a giant red explosion. Several days later as I was watching the Discovery program on television, I caught a glimpse of a space program showing a planet exploding. It was exactly the same picture as I had seen in this vision!

Now, God is giving me visions of His army and His angelic host on the move, going out before the people of God. I encourage you to refuse to be duped, as I had been by science fiction and atheism. Instead, become a friend of Jesus Christ and His full reality—please! All you have to do is open your mouth and say, "Jesus, I am sorry that I have not believed in You. Please come into my life today and be my Lord and Savior." And be welcomed to the awesome truth and reality of Christ.

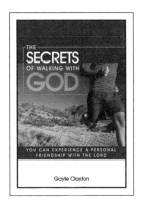

Additional copies of this book and other book titles from DESTINY IMAGE™ EUROPE are available at your local bookstore.

We are adding new titles every month!

To view our complete catalog online, visit us at:
www.eurodestinyimage.com

Send a request for a catalog to:

Via Acquacorrente, 6
65123 - Pescara - ITALY
Tel: +39 085 4716623 - Fax: +39 085 9431270

"Changing the world, one book at a time."

Are you an author?

Do you have a "today" God-given message?

CONTACT US

We will be happy to review your manuscript for the possibility of publication:

publisher@eurodestinyimage.com
http://www.eurodestinyimage.com/pages/AuthorsAppForm.htm